THIS STRANGE EVENTFUL HISTORY

THIS STRANGE EVENTFUL HISTORY

A PHILOSOPHY OF MEANING

PAIRS OF THINKERS IN PHILOSOPHY, RELIGION, SCIENCE AND ART

Paul Bradley

Algora Publishing
New York

Library of Congress Cataloging-in-Publication Data —

Bradley, Paul, 1935-
   This strange eventful history: a philosophy of meaning : pairs of thinkers in philosophy,
religion, science and art / Paul Bradley.
      p. cm.
   Includes bibliographical references and index.
      ISBN 978-0-87586-877-6 (alk. paper) — ISBN 978-0-87586-876-9 (soft cover:
alk. paper) — ISBN 978-0-87586-878-3 (ebook) 1. Meaning (Philosophy) 2. Meaning
(Philosophy)—Religious aspects. I. Title.
   B105.M4B69 2011
   128—dc23

                              2011023175

Printed in the United States

To my wife Carmen who enables all things for the author.

TABLE OF CONTENTS

PREFACE

All of us must seek at a personal and a general level for a philosophy of meaning in life, our "Strange Eventful History," as my fellow country-man Shakespeare described our existence. How can we logically plan and direct our personal philosophy if we do not know to what end—particularly in a world seemingly hell bent on destruction? The Existentialist philosophers cautioned that life is essentially meaningless but allowed that we may choose ourselves! Certainly, our choices are many and various in this current era. Often, however, we bemoan the lack of time to read and to research those possibilities. This book sets out to survey our options concisely, drawing on philosophy, religion, science and art. Each chapter takes two (or more) prominent inter-related thinkers to help us form an opinion, often provocatively. Philosophers who have experienced the Holocaust comment that those best adapted to survive life in concentration camps found an impetus in a purpose or a person to give them a meaning to hold onto. We must keep this carefully in mind. The Person may be a loved one or a religious archetypal figure.

The philosophy of religion (which appears to offer us ready-made meaning in its widest sense) is obviously a key subject, so we will review atheism, agnosticism, unifaith, interfaith, multifaith and transfaith (an attempt to define a new direction). Evolution, cosmology and re-thought intelligent design (are there blueprints behind life, akin to Plato's Forms, but not requiring an anthropomorphic Creator?) have an important place as do art and sensuality. Philosophy is clearly cardinal. Our direction is summarized as one of cosmic, compassionate plurality.

The approach is concise, pragmatic and non-scholarly, with short reading lists for the busy person. I too am busy—as a doctor wishing to be able to discuss matters of ultimate concern with my patients to help them find meaning in their plight and to identify a fulfilling pathway in my own life. I have been fortunate to travel widely, as a lecturer, enabling me to seek guidance from people of many backgrounds. The reader is indeed welcome to join me in a search for meaning in our privileged but sometimes daunting existence as conscious sentient beings in this extraordinary cosmos which we inhabit.

The caricatures that precede each chapter are free sketches by the author.

INTRODUCTION - SHAKESPEARE AND DON CUPITT

All the world's a stage, and all the men and women merely players; they have their exits and their entrances, and one man in his time plays many parts, his acts being seven ages. . . . Last scene of all, that ends this strange eventful history is second childishness and mere oblivion sans teeth, sans eyes, sans taste, sans everything.

—Shakespeare. "As You Like It," Jacques. Act II Scene 7.

AIMS

Shakespeare is a fellow Englishman and Midlander of mine, as I was born approximately 30 miles from Stratford upon Avon, his birthplace in leafy Warwickshire. As a boy, I frequently fished in the idyllic River Avon on whose banks the bard would have walked. Shakespeare had a unique ability to describe the human condition, but he appears to have taken care not to disclose too overtly his own deeper convictions about ultimate meaning in the world about him. There is little specific mention in his works of religion and personal philosophy. There was the ever present risk of finding one's head impaled on the gates to London Bridge (after the unspeakable horrors of being hanged, drawn and quartered) if one spoke out of turn in relationship to the current ruler's beliefs. The tension lay between the "Old Religion" of Catholicism incorporating the Latin Mass with the doctrine of the saints, versus Protestantism using the English Prayer Book and the plain table rather than the ornate altar. Shakespeare lived during turbulent times. His parents started their lives in the time of Queen Mary, a Catholic monarch (nicknamed Bloody Mary), while he is said to have produced his writings in the Protestant era of Queen Elizabeth and King James I. Was it all so important that the whole meaning of life hung on these specifics of religious doctrine? It was so important that Queen Elizabeth had been excommunicated by Pope Gregory XIII with a threat on her life and rumors of an ever-present risk of invasion by the Spanish armies of King Philip II! William needed to keep his head down as his mother came from a prominent Catholic family while his father, as mayor of Stratford, had to be seen to enforce sometimes draconian Protestant edicts. In my amateur acting days as a student, I acted in two of Shakespeare's plays, namely "Twelfth Night" (playing Malvolio, the priggish Steward), and "The Tempest" (Alonso, the treacherous King). In "The Tempest" (probably Shakespeare's last solo written play), one might possibly perceive a partly disguised figure of Deity in the form of the noble Prospero facing the responsibilities of taking care of all the inhabitants of his magical island from the ethereal Ariel to the brutish Caliban, surely an archetype of man's baser nature. It was a magical world Shakespeare chose, harking back to the old gods of the classical period avoiding the issues.

Shakespeare's seven ages of man span the mewling infant, the whining schoolboy, the sighing lover, the bearded, oathful soldier, the fat bellied justice and the lean and slippered pantaloon—a somewhat comical progression. At my time of life, I now face the not too far distant prospect of Shakespeare's last age:

> "Last scene of all, that ends this strange eventful history is second childishness and mere oblivion sans teeth, sans eyes, sans taste, sans everything." (As You Like It. Act II Scene 7)

This daunting stage of waning physical and mental faculties and the final epiphany of death have been a major stimulus to the world's philosophers, and theologians to find meaning and purpose in our existence when it may be seen to have such an ignominious end. That is our aim in this book. The search for meaning is an age-old one so that it may seem hopelessly naïve to set out on such a path—but more and more data almost daily becomes available to us. How can we guide our lives unless we have made an individual decision about the nature of our existence and our individual role—is it all essentially pointless or is new meaning slowly emerging?

In each chapter I have taken two or more related thinkers to help explore a particular topic and in the penultimate one this rises to four proponents! In this Introduction a second Englishman has been paired with Shakespeare namely Don Cupitt because his twenty first century view point challenges the legitimacy of our search in that he proposes forcefully, as an ex minister of the church, that the only thing on which to pronounce is Life itself: all else is pure invention of our own minds—more of him shortly!

The Difficulties Of Making A Start

Every morning while shaving I listen to People's Radio where one is confronted by the extraordinary complexity of the current world situation. One is reminded of the quotation:

"Chaos is order in the making." (Prigogine, 1997).

I hope and believe that this is possible but it requires an appropriate mind stance on the part of the human race to attempt to bring our world back into a meaningful equilibrium. The difficulty is to know where to start and finish in such a pursuit. The White Rabbit in *Alice in Wonderland* had a similar problem and was advised: "Begin at the beginning, and go on to the end: then stop" (Lewis Carroll, 1865).

But what is the beginning, and what could be the end? "That is the rub," to use a Shakespearian term. Undoubtedly it requires a historical approach, commencing with man's hominid predecessors and progressing to the various stages of *Homo habilis, Homo erectus, Homo neanderthalis*, leading up to *Homo sapiens*. This indeed is another "strange eventful history" in its prolonged plodding course over at least 4 million years. Why has it taken so long, and why has it been accompanied by such undoubted suffering? Do we see Hegel's slow emergence of spirit, or do we perceive it as in the eyes of Shakespeare's Macbeth?

"...a tale told by an idiot, full of sound and fury, signifying nothing." (Act V Scene 19)

It is always very difficult to start on a new creative effort. The writer stares at a blank sheet of paper gazing balefully back at him, as the painter confronts the uncompromising blank canvas in the effort to get started. I am reminded of the account by my fellow countryman, Winston Churchill of his difficulties in starting to paint in his delightful short monograph, *Painting as a Pastime*. He had been advised to take up this pursuit in 1915 to help him during the tribulation of a time when his services were not used by his country, despite the fact that he was aware of the growing German menace: "I knew everything but could do nothing." He had been invited to a country estate, and was set up under an umbrella confronting nature with a complete set of oils and a blank canvas in front of him. On such occasions Nature can present itself to one in a welter of detail from which it can be impossible to discern any kind of starting point. After being in this situation for some while, the gifted wife of his friend appeared and asked Winston how he was getting on. Winston indicated that nature in all its wonder was too difficult to render. In response she forcefully asked him, "But what are you hesitating about? Let me have a brush—the big one."

> Splash into the turpentine, wallop into the blue and white, frantic flourish on the palate—clean no longer—and then several large, fierce strokes and slashes of blue on the absolutely cowering canvas. Anyone could see that it could not hit back (Churchill, 1964).

Churchill narrated that the spell was broken and that sickly inhibitions rolled away. He seized the largest brush and "fell upon my victim with Berserk fury. I have never felt any awe of a canvas since."

So I too must take courage and attack the blank white paper!

Don Cupitt

Don Cupitt, our other Englishman, is as explicit in his views about the meaning of life as Shakespeare was implicit—but over four hundred years separate them in time and the penalties of speaking one's mind are much less! He started his career as a deacon in the Church of England in 1960 but progressively modified his outlook so that he now calls himself a non-realist humanist. His attitude to the existence of meaning or absence of such in life is clearly stated in this excerpt from his recent 2003 book *Life, Life*, in which he puts forward very forcefully the view that the only entity about which we can be certain is Life itself:

> There are in effect no meanings but human meanings and we can have no rational basis for claiming to detect signs of the purposes and activity of invisible non-human agencies. Our language simply does not and cannot give us the ability to tell rational certifiable tales about the doings of such beings. So we would do well to forget all about the meaning of life (Cupitt 2003).

As a result of these views, Cupitt quit his ministry in the Church becoming an academic, journalist and religious correspondent for the BBC. He is a prolific writer and the direction of his views can be gauged from such titles as *Taking Leave of God* and *Is Nothing Sacred? The Non-Realist Philosophy of Religion*. So one has to consider these very articulate and heartfelt views in any search for meaning, which Cupitt states does not exist! So that gives a little excitement to the contest!

Examining The Author's Credentials For The Task

At this stage, I must try to convince an intending reader that I have the necessary credentials to set out on such an ambitious path. After all, I am not a professional theologian, philosopher or historian, but a doctor! Let me be presumptuous and jot down some possible qualifications for the job in hand. The author Somerset Maugham stated, from his own personal experience, that there is no better training for a writer than to have practiced medicine, and I would agree: one confronts all aspects of human existence head on! After qualifying in England in medical school, it was necessary for me to work as an intern for six months each in general medicine and general surgery. Here, I became acquainted with the ultimate problem of death at first hand in my patients. As a medical student, I delivered thirty babies at a baby factory hospital in London's East End. So I am familiar with Shakespeare's first and last stages of life at first hand! Before graduating in medicine, I trained as a dentist. This gave me, amongst other things, an insight into the neurology of the head and neck region and the brain in particular. Brain function and the possibility of a mystical center in the nervous system will be one of our preoccupations in this book.

Before coming to the USA, where I now work as an academic, I was a professor at the Royal London Hospital in London's East End. This is the rough and tumble area of London where impecunious immigrants from all parts of the world have tended to settle initially. This acquainted me with suffering on the part of many of my patients from the hazards of unemployment, poor housing, and every kind of health problem, faced with great courage and a cockney sense of humor by the majority. Part of my work involved major head and neck injuries, many of them inflicted by fellow human beings with the utmost ferocity ("kicking the face in"), or self-inflicted by jumping under trains or from high buildings. How could such horrifying trauma be inflicted by a fellow human being or be self-inflicted? My other role lay in operating on cancer of the mouth and facial region—how does one view the presence of this evil crab-like growth transgressing the perfection of the body's tissues? It was enough to make or break a sufferer, but again the majority of patients rose to the challenge and seemed to achieve a deepening of character as a result. Where did they find their motivation? One learned from one's patients and wondered quietly how one might stand up to such a test oneself. Prior to this I was professor of my discipline in the glorious city of Edinburgh for eight years—the so-called "Venice of the North." This was the other side of life's coin, being in a place of privilege and beauty. So I have experienced the worst and the best. I have known some quite noble things, and I have also known some definitely ignoble ones!

As a university professor for over twenty-five years it has been my privilege to rub shoulders with colleagues of every other discipline of university life. I have been fortunate enough to lecture in over thirty countries and visit forty or more. Notable amongst these visits, have been four to India, and one to Nepal: this part of the world I regard as the true home of religion and philosophy. On such visits abroad, it has been my preoccupation to visit temples and churches and shrines and try to talk to people about their deepest feelings in far-flung parts of the world. I have never been very successful in making money in my career, but consider this privilege a more than adequate recompense!

While working in the University of Edinburgh, I undertook a three year part time diploma course in Philosophy and Religion. In this course, I was taught by some very remarkable theologians and philosophers and by one major figure in the field of Inter Faith dialogue, Dr. Frank Whaling. All of this opened my mind, and I am totally thankful to those teachers for the influence they had on a perplexed mind. After completing the necessary essays and exams, they gave me my diploma at the end but I detected perhaps a little reluctance for I surmised that they feared that I might be a heretic of some sort! I think that may be true, but I can only state that I confront life with a feeling of reverence and awe coupled with a conviction that meaning may be found if the mind is unbiased and totally open to truth. I had lost my original faith of Christianity largely due to its attitude of exclusivity (salvation is only possible within this one tradition), and had joined the University Buddhist Society. This, together with the course, helped tremendously for I acquired a new philosophy of meaning, a fresh iconology, a fellowship and the possibility to put the entity of a "personal God" in the pending tray. Buddhism against the background of Inter Faith dialogue allows this freedom. We will look at both topics in detail in the coming pages as they helped me greatly to redefine meaning and can aid others, I feel sure, in a new start.

Conclusion: The Thinker

I hope that an intending reader does not feel that I have too much presumption in accompanying him or her in this search for ultimate meaning, for that would be my working definition of both philosophy and religion. I feel empathy with Socrates who at a similar stage in his life stated:

"I now know one thing, namely that I know nothing!"

By that, I think he meant that his mind was full of a host of superficialities but that at this time in his existence he needed to make a synthesis from them. So do I! We need to consider the wide variety of ways of viewing this puzzling, intriguing, beautiful, fierce world and life of ours and finding a view point appropriate to a thinking and caring person. As illustration to this section I have used an image of Rodin's "Le Penseur." The agonized concentration on the face of The Thinker illustrates man's predicament. And of course Rodin originally perceived this portrayal to be part of his great work, "The Gates of Hell," which took him nearly forty years to complete. Perhaps Rodin feared facing a penalty for the sensuality portrayed so brilliantly in his sculpture. The Gates of Hell illustrate allegorically, in a Christian perspective, the penalty for getting it all wrong. That must concentrate the mind in our journey. However, we are going to attempt to widen our perspective to take in all faiths, both theistic and non-theistic, and philosophies both religious and non-religious.

Let us start our search with the existentialist viewpoint which is as uncompromising as that of Don Cupitt.

Reading List and Sources
Life, Life. Don Cupitt. Polebridge Press 2003.
Will in the World. Stephen Greenblatt. W.W. Norton and Co 2004.

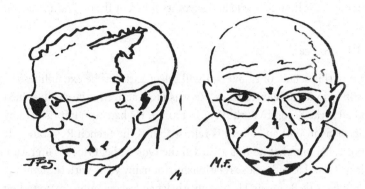

CHAPTER 1. THE DEFAULT STANCE OF EXISTENTIALISM AND POST MODERNISM

Jean Paul Sartre and Michael Foucault

Question: Do Existentialism and Post Modernism
wipe the slate clean and provide a challenging
starting point for our search for meaning?

THE BLANK CANVAS

We seek a blank canvas as the background on which to trace a picture of life from whence we set out to derive meaning. In the Introduction, Winston Churchill was instanced with his difficulty in starting to portray the bewildering detail of nature on his first canvas. Once he had learned that he could attack the bare surface, he never looked back in his endeavors. The philosophical school of existentialism provides us with a similar metaphorical starting point or blank canvas. The existentialist chain of thought encompasses the names Kierkegaard, Nietzsche, Husserl, Heidegger, Sartre, De Beauvoir, and Camus in approximate chronological order. Their essential message is that man is alone is a godless world for which there is no meaning as such. Kierkegaard stressed the role of the individual in this austere situation trying to rescue a place for religion in a rethought mode. For the others, as with most modern philosophers, religion was however archaic. Heidegger made a plea for the phenomenological attitude whereby one should be totally non-judgmental in viewing another man's philosophy, but merely let it flow over you and savor its inherent flavor. Let us take on that attitude.

Jean Paul Sartre

Out of this school of thinkers, I will select Sartre as he exemplifies the philosophy in its developed form. He was most active in the disillusioned period after the Second World War in France. He had been imprisoned by the Germans in 1941 and after his release joined the French Resistance. It was typical of him that he was awarded the 1964 Nobel Prize for literature but declined it. He had a close relationship for many years with the feminist writer Simone de Beauvoir. He was an atheist and a communist expounding his views with great fervor. He emphasized strongly that life is "nothing" indeed it is a" nothingness" with no meaning to be found. This is really a default position in philosophy. He did however emphasize that man could "choose himself." In other words he could select a mind stance or attitude provided he realized it had no inherent meaning. This allows us at least a starting point on our journey!

Nausea: The Novel

This Sartre work was written in 1938 in the fateful year before the commencement of hostilities of the Second World War. It perfectly illustrates the workings of the disillusioned mind. The central character, Roquentin, is a writer himself but is unable to work because he experiences a disabling nausea for life around him. He spends most of his time in the small French fishing town of Bouville. Ostensibly, this is an attractive environment with the old city, its gardens, and the ocean. He acknowledges that he is alone and free, but the freedom is rather like death to him:

> I am bored, that's all. It is a profound boredom, profound, the profound heart of existence, the very matter I am made of.

> There is absolutely no more reason for living, all the ones I have tried have given way, and I can't imagine any more of them." (Sartre 1938)

Everything and everyone that he sees evoke in him a feeling of revulsion. He goes into the local museum to view portraits and statues of local worthies of a previous generation, but is overwhelmed by their pomposity. Even the sight of the root of an ancient tree is almost obscene to him.

We must all of us recognize this sort of thought ourselves from time to time. The chaos of the current world position is enough to evoke them in itself unless we have inner resources. Roquentin does finally regain a sense of purpose when he is able to resume writing.

POST MODERNISM

There is a certain arid cleansing beauty about existentialist thought. It is on this bleak foundation that the school of Post Modernist thought is built, with such names as Claude Levi-Strauss, Michael Foucault, and Jacques Derrida. Post Modernism is even more disturbing in that it puts in doubt all previous philosophical thought. It has been called "anti-foundational" in that is represents a deep skepticism about authority, received wisdom, cultural and political norms. The German existentialist philosopher Frederic Nietzsche had called for a "re-evaluation of all values" and this has been seen as a battle cry for the eventual Post Modern movement. Language itself was questioned in its validity in a series of steps of logical analysis, logical positivism, and logical atomism. Derrida for example demands a strategy of deconstruction whereby language must be ruthlessly explored to reveal the multiple meanings unconsciously at war with each other in any text. It is indeed *The Waste Land*" to use the title of T.S. Eliot's great but daunting poem.

MICHEL FOUCAULT

Foucault was a central figure in the Post Modern Movement bringing to his work the skills of the philosopher, the historian and the cultural critic. Typical of this movement, he viewed the apparent progress of modernity with considerable skepticism. The modern viewpoint was an assumption that the quality of life could indefinitely be improved under the influence of science and technology but two world wars had shattered this illusion of inevitable progress. Foucault's viewpoint was dark and pessimistic but he felt that philosophy, correctly conceived, was a possible means of redressing the imbalance of the world. He held the post of Professor of the History of Systems of Thought at the College de France from 1970 to 1984. The title of his post illustrates his attitude which was to determine how apparent truths have changed over the centuries from age to age and culture to culture. His book *The Order of Things* (1966) was a best seller in France. In it he explored the fields of psychiatry, medicine, biology, linguistics and economics emphasizing how these disciplines seek to carve the world into apparently ordered, controllable units fixing each of them into a rigid structure. Authority using the tools of power and knowledge attempts to force conformity on the individual by setting out to:

- classify
- dominate
- exclude
- exploit

He felt he must use an archaeological approach and indeed one of his books is entitled *The Archaeology of Knowledge* (1969). It is necessary to go right back to the beginning of a topic and disinter the original bones of the subject much as an archeologist digs up the artifacts of long past civilizations. Knowledge, in the form of theories, can change very radically but those very theories have a sinister power over the individual. This viewpoint is very similar to the later philosophy of Thomas Kuhn who pointed out that there are radical discontinuities between different periods of scientific investigation: he called these disparate paradigms. It is vital to reexamine what we think we know in the light of the effect that knowledge has on our lives. Foucault stated that we must investigate: "A history of the different modes by which...human beings are made subjects" (Foucault 1969).

Foucault's Key Books

With this in mind, he set out to conduct a series of historical investigations into particular institutions in the following seminal books:

- *Madness and Civilization* (1961):

Here he examined the treatment of the insane from the end of the Middle Ages through the Age of Reason to modernity. He claimed that in the eighteenth century for example "madness" was used to stigmatize not just those who were mentally ill but also the poor, the sick, the homeless and anyone whose lack of conformity to social norms was deemed inappropriate. One is mindful of the fact that in communist Russia, political dissidents were often placed in asylums as a means of taking them out of society to reduce their impact.

- *Discipline and Punishment* (1975):

Here he reviewed the historical development of the treatment of another estranged member of the community namely the criminal. He narrated the transition from the brutal treatment of criminals under feudal regimes to the more diffuse and apparently effective forms of social control in modern society. Here the emphasis changed from using the body as an element of control or coercion to the use of the mind itself. However there was always the emphasis on exerting vengeance rather than trying to help him or her to reintegrate into society. All too often a period in prison strengthened criminal resolve rather than supporting an effort to live a new reformed life.

• *History of Sexuality* (1976 to 1984):

Despite occupying three volumes this great project was still unfinished at his untimely death at the age of 58. Foucault was desperately concerned that sexual norms in society could seek to enforce conformity on an individual. He presented a history or archeology of sexual behavior contrasting the Greek acceptance of boy love to the early Christian concern with marriage and heterosexual relations. As a homosexual, he knew very well the harshness of society's judgment of what was natural and unnatural. Sadly, Foucault's life was cut short when he died from Acquired Immune Deficiency Syndrome (AIDS) in 1984.

Foucault's post modern method as a philosopher, historian, and cultural critic can help us in our journey by using his concept of the archeology of a subject to allow its proper historical evaluation. It encourages us to disentangle knowledge from the power that it may exert in society in an unjust manner. It provides warnings for us if we cannot, as a species, find a meaningful sense of purpose in life. One of Foucault's most famous sayings sounds a cautionary note: "Man is a recent invention who could be erased like a face drawn in the sand at the edge of the sea" (Foucault 1976).

That note concentrates the mind impressively.

VIKTOR FRANKL — A REBUTTAL OF EXISTENTIALISM

Viktor Frankl MD PhD (1905 to 1997—a very long life) was someone who was not prepared to accept the reductionism of the existentialists—the "existential vacuum" as he termed it. You will not find him featured in many texts on philosophy being best known as an eminent psychiatrist and neurologist and even occasional neurosurgeon—indeed a rare combination of talents. These took him to the position of Director of the Vienna Polyclinic with eventual professorships in the University of Vienna and as a visitor at Harvard. He was Jewish spending three years in Auschwitz, Dachau and other concentration camps during World II: his wife and parents were killed in the camps while he only survived because his talents were used to treat depression and prevent suicide. He came to realize that those inmates with the optimal mental attitude to allow them to withstand the terrible rigors of the situation were those who wished to survive to fulfill a future goal or for the sake of certain people who gave them a sense of meaning. The people were usually loved ones waiting for them. Let me quote him from *The Unheard Cry for Meaning*, a later one of his 32 books (1978) on the question of existential reductionism:

> Reductionism is the nihilism of today. It is true that Jean-Paul Sartre's brand of existentialism hinges on the pivots "Being and Nothingness" but the lesson to be learned from existentialism is a hyphenated nothingness, namely the no-thingness of the human being. A human being is not one thing among other things. Things determine each other. Man, however determines himself. Rather he decides whether or not he lets himself be determined, be it by the drives and instincts that push him, or the reasons and meanings that pull him (Frankl, 1978).

It can be appreciated that he also fought against the concepts of behaviorism as expounded by Burrhus Skinner. Skinner explained all human behavior on the basis of "operant conditions," which are environmental stimuli that have reinforcing or adverse effects as one might observe in an experimental animal. Frankl had personal experience of human beings under the worst conditions possible and they didn't behave like that—Man exhibited control of his actions in the form of what he termed "Pandeterminism." He came to the conclusion that there are two races of men even in extremis, namely decent and non-decent ones, or saints and swine He used his observations to found a school of treatment which he termed Logotherapy—the third Viennese School of Psychotherapy after Freud's Psychoanalysis with its emphasis on the Will to Satisfaction and Adler's Individual Psychology emphasizing the Will to Power. Logotherapy on the other hand concentrates on the Will to Meaning—the aim of our present search! So Frankl is a very seminal figure for us.

Frankl's Bestseller: "Man's Search for Meaning"

In 1959, Frankl authored this book whose subject obviously met a very real inner need on the part of the reading public—more than 12 million copies are in print worldwide ! I was unable to borrow one of the two copies in my university library as they never appeared on the shelves but seemed to be handed from one reader to another in continuum, indicating the ever fresh appeal of the work. Equally telling was the fact that my local book-seller kept a very low cost soft cover version immediately available—not bad for a publication 50 years from its innovation. I read my copy from cover to cover in one day, attesting to its clear style and absorbing qualities. Only after I had nearly completed this book did it come to my notice that I had made a most important omission in view of Frankl's major contribution on the subject. Frankl narrates his experience in the camps, where men were robbed of all identity by being shaved of every vestige of body hair, dressed in foul rags and identified only by a number. They were subjected to every form of meaningless brutality and completely isolated from all contact with the world outside the unbelievable grimness of their surroundings. Death was an ever present possibility—only one in twenty-eight would survive. Here was suffering at its most extreme, and yet Frankl could discern mean-ing there, in that it could be a stimulus to spiritual growth. He quotes Dos-toevsky: "There is one thing I dread, not to be worthy of my sufferings." Frankl sums it up:

> These words frequently came to my mind after I became acquaint-ed with those martyrs whose behavior in camp, whose suffering and death, bore witness to the fact that the last inner freedom cannot be lost. It can be said that they were worthy of their sufferings; the way they bore their suffering was a genuine inner achievement. It is this spiritual freedom—which cannot be taken away—that makes life meaningful and purposeful. (Frankl 1959)

This was my own conclusion after observing the heroism shown by the majority of my patients confronting terminal head and neck cancer. Frankl's book is essential reading for any student of meaning and purpose in human existence.

Does Religion Have Any Role In The Discussion?

Existentialism and Post Modernism provide a provocative start in our search for meaning even though Frankl shows their limitations on the basis of pure experience. They cannot be ignored and indeed they are the underly-ing reductionist theme of modern philosophy. Religion offers an apparent antidote for this astringent medicine and promises us meaning. However, it is very easy to be put off religion by much of its quasi-magical, mythical basis when it is presented by fundamentalists. Its antidotal properties still have a great allure for all of us who appear perplexed and lost in a world of chaos. Let me call on Shakespeare again through the words of Polonius: "This above all, to thine own self be true, and it must follow as the night the day thou canst not then be false to any man" (Hamlet Act I Scene 3).

Is religion a dangerous seductive force to make us false to our own selves by accepting something, because of its reassuring qualities, that we know deep within ourselves is untrue? We must not ignore the immense role that religion has played in man's history both for good and evil. Every human group will produce a religion in the same way that it will invent language, music, and art. It appears to be hard wired into the human psyche. Do we need to deprogram it, or is it more appropriate to reprogram it into a new Post Modern form? These are vital subjects for us to examine remembering that we have been told we can at least "choose ourselves" in the existentialist world. We can choose to view the world religiously, but what will that do to us, and what religion will we select? Can we garner from the world religions their essential meanings and forge a new religion for this Post Modern era? We will look at various ways of expressing religion, each exemplified by a dialogue of individual men, at the end of this text. Before we come to that, it is the plan to seek evidence from philosophy, the atheist view point, the sensualist view point, the view of mysticism, the agnostic stand, the primatologist, and the neuroscientist. It is the intention to be brief and succinct in the approach but we do need evidence to ponder and evaluate.

Answer: Yes, Existentialism and Post Modernism do allow us to choose our own path to Meaning without preconceptions. We must keep in mind Frankl's pointers to personal meaning in the form of a Goal or a Person.

Reading List and Sources

Existentialism and Humanism. Jean Paul Sartre. Methuen. 2007.

Postmodern Thought. Edited by Stuart Sim. Icon Books. 1998

Man's Search for Ultimate Meaning. Viktor Frankl. Boston Press. 1959. 2006.

CHAPTER 2. THE CLASSICAL PHILOSOPHERS

Socrates and the Buddha

Question: Is it possible that these two BCE Philosophers formulated important concepts that are meaningful in our modern era?

PHILOSOPHIA: THE LOVE OF WISDOM

Wisdom is what we crave in our search for a meaningful attitude in life. In the East, wisdom is equated with age so that the elder person is expected to be a philosopher and is honored as such. In the West, this may not be the case, so that the senior person may be viewed as a silly old man or a silly old woman, unless, of course, his or her wallet is large enough to make their opinion important to others! This may be our own fault because in modern life, philosophy may take a second place to materialistic interests and aims. In the West philosophy commenced around the sixth century before the Common Era. The proud father in the current film, "My Big Fat Greek Wedding," states that "we invented philosophy" together with a lot of other claims, and he was partly right! It has been stated that all philosophy is merely footnotes to Plato (Alfred North Whitehead). So we must give special attention to the "big three"—Socrates, Plato, Aristotle. All the major questions of existence were examined by this seminal trio. Having said this, we must remember an equally early, or even earlier, start of philosophical thought in the east, so that we will examine the contribution of the Buddha later.

THE PRE-SOCRATICS: XENOPHANES

Before we come to the big three, let us think about the Pre-Socratics who were dispersed around the Greek Empire from around 600 to 400 B.C.E. They started the debate although many of their writings are fragmentary. Let us select from this period Xenophanes (560-478 B.C.E.) because he had some very provocative and very innovative views on the nature of Deity, or in a more abstract sense, the possibility of Intelligence behind all life. He lived for a period in Elea, a Greek colony in southern Italy founded by refugees to the area due to the advance of Persia into the Aegean. If we are to seek ultimate meaning in life, it is obviously very important to debate whether intelligence lies behind its creation or whether it is truly meaningless as in the existentialist claim. In paraphrase, this is what Xenophanes had to say: "If horses had hands and could draw, they would draw pictures of Gods like horses" (Jaeger 1936).

Xenophanes was reacting against the image of the pantheon of Greek Gods as described by Homer in the Iliad and the Odyssey. Xenophanes felt it was illogical to worship such gods because they all behaved irrationally and immorally. He was commenting that we tend to image Deity in human-like forms i.e. anthropomorphic form. He implied that this was due to a lack of imagination on our part. We will discuss other images for intelligence later, particularly when we bring in the views of John Hick, a noted Inter Faith writer. It is still true that this type of imaging relates to the great monotheistic religions of this present day, namely Judaism, Christianity, and Islam. Intelligence can all too easily be thought of in the terms of an Old Man in the Sky—a mental image which tends to be epitomized by Michelangelo's portrayal of God touching Adam's finger in the Sistine Chapel. This is an inspiring portrayal but perfectly illustrates Xenophanes' point!

THE BIG THREE: SOCRATES, PLATO, AND ARISTOTLE

We tend to think of these three great figures functioning in a time of academic calm. When we view the Parthenon in Athens, it seems to speak of certainty and solidity. However, the fifth century B.C.E was very different from this. It was a time to equal our own for its feeling of insecurity and threat for those who lived in Athens. The great City State had been defeated by Sparta. Its charismatic leader Pericles was dead from the plague, its city walls were breached and control had gone to a group of Tyrants.

This is the kind of background that creates an acute need for "Philosophia" or "Wisdom"!

Socrates, the mentor of the other two, illustrates the strength of feeling and action which religion can provoke. He chose to take the Hemlock to die for his religious beliefs. What was his crime? It was stated to comprise not recognizing the official state Gods, and allegedly polluting the youth of Athens with his views. This is the archetypal situation where two groups of people are so convinced by their own imaging that on the one hand, they are prepared to kill for it, and on the other hand, an individual may elect to be a martyr to his views. Socrates could not agree with the conventional picture of the gods which were mainly concerned with warring and whoring! On Plato's testimony, he was however a very religious man and had a touching regard for Pan, the god of nature, and Asclepius the god of medicine. In the latter context, one turns one's mind to Hippocrates, the founder of medicine living in this era whose great statement echoes in our ears in this time: "Life is short, the Art is long, Opportunity fleeting, Experiment dangerous and Judgment difficult" (Porter 1999).

He was of course talking of medicine, but this statement could be extended to life itself!

The views of Plato and Aristotle became much more abstract in the relationship to Intelligence. Plato, an early Rationalist, had an image of a God of Gods, who he called "the Framer." He set life going, but left it to the young gods to create nature and mould mortal bodies for man (the concept of a Demiurge) as expounded in the Timaeus. Aristotle, his pupil, had an even more abstract idea. He was a very early Empiricist. He did not believe in Plato's theory of the Forms, which lay outside the world of men acting as ideals or templates for such qualities as the Good, Beauty and Truth. Aristotle had a concept of Essence lying within and not outside the human sphere. His image of intelligence was of the Unmoved Mover. This Intelligence lay outside the normal sphere of man, and probably the Cosmos—it "thought itself" but did not involve itself in the day-to-day life of the world. It was an idea revived in the history of world religion in the eighteenth century Enlightenment concept of the Deists who thought of Deity as an influence that wound up the clock of life but then left it to tick on its own without interference...

The Theory Of The Forms (Or Universals And Particulars)

Let us examine this theory described by Plato in the Republic and defended by Socrates in the Parmenides. It is a totally fascinating concept developed mainly by intuition which can be related to Jung's twentieth century theory of the Archetypes and most recently to the idea of Intelligent Design as expounded by Hoyle—we will be examining both of these later. It is always difficult to decide whether any teaching such as this originated from Socrates or Plato because Socrates never recorded his thoughts, preferring active dialogue, so that we rely on Plato's writings where Socrates is featured as a major spokesman (Plato never featured himself!). As in many teacher–pupil relationships, we can assume that they spoke with basically the same voice. Certainly, they were both Rationalists using Reason and inner contemplation to derive conclusions as opposed to outside observations from the senses relied upon by the Empiricist school exemplified by their successor Aristotle. The division between Rationalism and Empiricism is probably the greatest divide in Philosophy only reconciled by Immanuel Kant in the eighteenth century who stated, very sensibly, that both viewpoints could be combined with good effect!

The Theory proposes that the objects in the outer world about us (the Particulars) which we are aware of through our senses of vision, touch ,hearing, smell and taste (the Sentient World) and also our faculty of thought are representations of more purified objects, the Forms or Ideas, in another sphere outside time and space. In a more modern sense, these could be described as Blue Prints or Templates. The properties of the Forms have been summarized as:

- They are pure qualities whereas an individual particular object may be a mixture of say shape, size, color and texture. There is a Form of Circularity, for instance, which is perfect in its shape and symmetry whereas an individual object may not be perfectly round
- They are the perfect models or Archetypes on which the objects of the outer world are based in their particulars.
- They are the underlying causes for the particulars to which they owe their existence.
- They provide order and intelligibility to the objects.
- They are Transcendent.

- The major Forms are Truth, Beauty, Justice and underlying them all the supreme one of the Good.
- There is a hierarchy from lowest to highest comprising Images, Material Objects, Lower Forms, Higher Forms and finally the Form of the Good.
- They are Unchanging being in total contrast to the flux and changeability of the things of our outer world.
- Forms have a far greater reality and vividness when appreciated than the mundane occupants of our day to day existence.

How can we train ourselves to see beyond the Particulars to the underlying Forms? By "Knowledge," we are told. The more we learn with an honest mind the more the veil will be lifted. Our gift for this all consuming effort will be to come to recognize Truth, Beauty, Justice and as the supreme reward the nature of the Good to which all else is subservient This is known in Philosophy as an Idealist position. Plato also made the wonderfully mysterious comment "knowing is remembering" hinting that in a previous state we had actually come face to face with the Forms (anamnesis)! Socrates taught by the Dialectical Method where he would probe the mind of his subject stimulating him to express his opinions so that these could be carefully dissected. Frequently two opposing views would emerge, a thesis and an anti-thesis,—the challenge would then be to resolve these into an overarching synthesis. In one sense, the Particulars and the Forms can produce a synthesis in the enlightened mind. We will return to the concept of the Forms in the next section on Buddhism and in our final chapter as it can be adapted to consideration of the fascinating topic of Intelligent Design.

ARISTOTLE AND THE SEARCH FOR PURPOSE (TELOS) AND MEANING

We must consider Aristotle further in our search for Meaning for he was preoccupied with probing for purpose in the phenomena that he examined—the bust by Lysippos, in the Louvre, brilliantly portrays the keenness of his gaze. Aristotle was concerned with particulars rather than any concept of underlying forms characterizing his reliance on sense data as the keynote of his empiricist attitude. The breadth of his interests was staggering embracing biology, astronomy, psychology, physics, ethics, logic, metaphysics, politics, and justice. Always, he was not content to describe and categorize (although he did this with scientific fervor) but looked further into the teleological aspects: that is, he sought an underlying cause. Typical is his classification of the *aitia* of an object under examination which came to be known as the four causes:

1. Material: its bodily constituents.
2. Efficient: the means which brought it into existence.
3. Formal: its pattern or formula.
4. Final: its end.

The final cause brings in the concept of a goal or interpretation in terms of final purpose or teleology. The ultimate Telos lies in its relationship to the underlying basis of existence and even the Unmoved Mover. This attitude is the antithesis of modern scientific reasoning which does not look for meaning save in the case of rare individuals such as the cosmologist Sir Fred Hoyle, on whom we concentrate at length in a later chapter because he had the courage to seek the Intelligence which he considered lay behind the structure of existence and the cosmos itself. Always there is the resolution of thesis versus antithesis to produce a reasoned synthesis—the dialectic. Aristotle in the Metaphysics stated that "all human beings have a natural desire for knowledge." He conceded that even "the lover of myth is a kind of philosopher" but he looked beyond the myth as we must do.

CONCLUSION

The dialectical method also has had great influence particularly in the philosophies of Hegel and Carl Marx. These are all challenging ideas and have a modem feel to them. We must not however be too set in the idea of the Greeks inventing philosophy, for there were similar ideas going around in Asia, and the Indian subcontinent in particular. They relate to the so-called Axial Period in which great thinkers arose in various parts of the world. It may even be that Eastern views predated those in the West!

THE BUDDHA

The Axial Age

The concept of an Axial Age around the fifth and sixth centuries BCE was introduced by the German philosopher, Karl Jaspers (Jaspers 1977). During this time a number of major thinkers arose around the world surveying their current situation and coming up with new solutions to man's spiritual status. The actual extent of the axial age has now been extended considerably from around nine hundred to two hundred B.C.E. Socrates in the fifth century B.C.E was a pivotal figure in Greek Philosophy. In China Confucius and Lao Tzu presented the schools of Confucianism and Taoism respectively. In the Middle East, the second Isaiah and Ezekiel in the Abrahamic tradition were major figures. The Buddha was a pivotal voice in this Axial Age. The dates of his life have been suggested approximately as 563 to 483 BCE. As with many such figures of antiquity, these times are conjectural. Philosophers and historians in the Indian subcontinent stress the earlier dates pointing out that Indian philosophy may have pre-dated much of Greek Philosophy! On the other hand, western observers have tended to displace the Buddha into a later era and this is particularly true of those speaking during the Colonial Age when there were great reservations about conceding that the colonized lands may have had more advanced philosophy before the western world!

The Life of the Buddha

The Buddha was reputedly born as Siddhartha Gotama, the son of the leader of the Shakya Tribe in the Gangetic plain in the area at the junction between Nepal and India. It is held that he lived a life of great luxury in his father's palace—indeed his father was at pains to shelter him from the outer world as it had been predicted that his son could be either a great temporal leader or a great spiritual leader. His father feared the latter option although that was what came to be. Siddhartha covertly managed to go beyond the boundaries of the palace thanks to the secret efforts of his charioteer. In those illicit journeys he experienced the so called "Four Sights." The first three of these brought him face to face with human suffering in the form of an old man, a sick man, and a dead man. This is said to have shattered his composure and left him in mental turmoil as to why such suffering should exist. However, he then saw, as his fourth sight, a wandering ascetic (a Sanyasin) dressed in a yellow robe and seeming to show great tranquility. Siddhartha realized that this was going to be the only course open to him if he was to settle the unrest in his mind. In the dead of night, he crept out of the palace leaving his beautiful wife and young baby to go forth into the outside world. This was the so called "Great Departure." He exchanged his royal garb with a passing beggar. He then joined a group of other young Sanyasins and enrolled himself with two teachers in succession. Neither of them satisfied his longings and he realized that he must find his own solution within. He tried to clear his mind by reducing the food that he took down to a proverbial one grain of rice a day. This was counterproductive as he found that he could not think clearly. He realized that he must reach a so called "Middle Way." He started to take enough food for his minimal needs and found that this helped him. He started to meditate on four aspects of life:

- The Impermanence of all Life
- The Interdependence of All Forms of Life (Karma)
- The Universality of Suffering
- The Problem of Ignorance

The Great Enlightenment

Finally one dawn, while sitting under a great pipal tree (the so called Bodhi Tree) he is said to have achieved the insight of the so called "Great Enlightenment." He came upon, within himself, what he termed "a path of great antiquity traveled by human beings in a far off distant era." *(Maijima Nikaya. Pali Canon)*

The site of his enlightenment is now commemorated at Bodh Gaya where there is still an ancient pipal tree and a great temple. He was tempted to keep his new found insight to himself but overcame this temptation realizing that he must preach this to the world around him. He assembled five of his previous companions in an ancient deer park near present day Benares and preached to them the so called "First Sermon." They had previously deserted him in view of his uncertainty of mind but now sat around him impressed by his new found certainty.

The Four Noble Truths

He now saw that the problem within his mind could be addressed by what have become known as the Four Noble Truths which he expressed as:

- Life is Suffering (the Sanskrit word is Dukka).
- The cause of suffering is Attachment (Tanha).
- It is possible to counteract the suffering by achieving a mental state of tranquility (Nirvana).
- This is achieved by following a Path (the Dharma).

This message may come across to us strongly in a materialistic world. It is all too easy to show attachment to possessions, people around us who we feel should behave towards us in a particular way, our position in the world. We can become attached to our health feeling that we have an entitlement to fitness and may be destroyed mentally if this is not so. We may, by extension, be attached to the concept of a Personal God and be shattered if he does not answer our prayers. It is indeed good news that we can escape that suffering if we can eliminate attachment and achieve a mental state of tranquility termed Nirvana.

Siddhartha was a little reluctant to define Nirvana stressing that is was an ineffable concept but many descriptions have subsequently been given as follows:

• The term literally means a Blowing Out as when a candle flame is extinguished although the energy, of course, is never lost.
• A Far Shore.
• The Security.
• Refuge.
• Peace.
• The Unfading.
• The Undecaying, Unaging, Undying, Unsorrowing, Unborn.
• The Stronghold.

One can achieve Nirvana, by following a path (the Eight Fold Path).

The Eightfold Path

The elements of the Eight Fold Path are:
• Right (or Correct)View
• Right Thought
• Right Speech
• Right Conduct
• Right Livelihood.
• Right Effort
• Right Mindfulness
• Right Concentration

These eight components can be summarized under three headings mainly Morality (Sila), Meditation (Samadhi), and Wisdom (Prana).

This is combined with the so called Five Precepts which are:
• No killing
• No stealing
• No sexual misconduct
• No lying
• No intoxicants

The Unanswered Questions (Avyakata) and Skillful Means (Upaya)

It is inevitable that Siddhartha was subjected to penetrating questions by his early and later followers and particularly the following:

- Is the world eternal?
- Is the world infinite?
- Is the soul identical with the body?
- Does the Buddha exist after death?

Siddhartha has been known as the Buddha (the Enlightened One) after his great insight. He replied that we do not need to know the answers to the above questions which he called the Avyakata. We do not need this information to be able to lead a good a life which is embraced in the Four Noble Truths. It is easy to see that the early Buddhism was a form of noble pragmatism, which quickly allowed followers to set out on a new sense of meaning for their lives without being encumbered by the need to acquire extensive didactic knowledge.

The Buddha's Path required also so called Skillful Means (Upaya) to achieve each stage on the spiritual journey. He told the parable of the Raft in which a man uses a raft to cross a large expanse of water. When he reaches the further side he has to decide whether to discard the raft or to carry it as a burden on his shoulder until he comes upon the next stretch of water as a barrier to his progress. The Buddha suggested that he should put aside the raft and find a new one at the new juncture. In other words, one must be prepared to find new insight as each stage on life's journey as enlightenment comes in steps.

The Concept of No Self (Anatta)

Undoubtedly the most shattering of the Buddha's demands is that we should give up attachment to our concept of an inner Self (the Ego as it was later termed by Freud). The Buddha taught that the self is merely a combination of the so called five Skandas which are:

- Corporeality
- Sensation
- Perception
- Volitional Formations
- Consciousness

It is this inner Self which seeks to attach itself to possessions, money, people, and position. It is the greatest obstacle to our identifying with other members of our species and indeed all feeling creatures in the world (Sentient Beings). Modern neuropsychiatry has tended to come to a similar conclusion attributing our sense of self to an ever changing relationship between our brain centers particularly the higher cognitive center in the prefrontal cortex, the center for memory in the hippocampus, the emotional center in the amygdala and the switching mechanism in the pallidum. The eighteenth-century Scottish philosopher David Hume (Hume 1748), came to a similar conclusion feeling that the self is simply a "bundle of perceptions." Aldous Huxley, the twentieth-century writer, pointed out in his influential text *The Perennial Philosophy* (Huxley 1977) that full spiritual development requires the step of "self naughting." Arthur Schopenhauer in the nineteenth century was an influential philosopher with definitely Buddhist leanings. His major text *The World as Will and Idea* defined the all powerful Will initiated by the Self. (Schopenhauer 1818) To elude its tyrannical hold, the individual needed to escape into the Arts, particularly music, and practice the identification of the Self with Another.

Mindfulness: Meditation

The Buddha had achieved his Enlightenment through prolonged Meditation—a process of Mindfulness. Meditation is a central aspect of Buddhism which has increased in importance as it has developed and has been taken on by other traditions. It has much to offer us as we ponder meaning. We can define the following components of the meditative process namely:

• Posture (Asana). It is necessary to achieve a completely relaxed position, ideally in the Lotus or semi-Lotus position, but these alternatives are not essential. It is sufficient to sit in a comfortable position. Place the hands on the lap with the palms upwards—this is the posture or *mudra* of meditation and has a remarkable relaxant effect. Please try it, if it is new to you!

• Control of Breath (Pranayama). Concentration on slow rhythmic breathing is central to the process. It should be noted that physiologically altering oxygen intake and carbon dioxide output in this way will have effects on cerebral perfusion and conscious state.

• One Point Attention (Ekagrata). The attention should be centered on some outside object to still fleeting thoughts in the brain. The object should be viewed without trying to form any judgmental conceptions but simply drinking in its inner aspect. A natural object such as a plant or stone is ideal.

• The Four Jhanas (the Trance States). Training allows the adept to go through a succession of trance states but these should not be sought too early in one's progress.

• The Four Ayatanas (Meditative States). To achieve these states, requires long practice and often advice from an advanced meditative practitioner (a Guru).

There are various aids to achievement of mindfulness such as the use of:

• Mandelas. These are sacred diagrams, often of an abstract nature.

• Mantras. These are chants of various sorts whose rhythmic nature helps to program the mind. A classical one developed in later Tantric Buddhism is that invoking the spirit of Compassion, namely: *Om Mani Padme Hum.*

• Contemplation of the Four Great Virtues (the Bramaviharas). These are:

a) Benevolence.

b) Compassion.

c) Joy in the Joy of Others.

d) Equanimity.

The Propagation of Buddhism: King Asoka

King Asoka ruled India between 273 to 232 BCE: he greatly extended the Indian Mauryan Empire with a series of bloody conquests. He was then said to have been overcome by remorse and found consolation in Buddhism. This story was popularized in the recent film "Asoka." He revived and restored historical Buddhist sites throughout India and set up great pillars with Buddhist inscriptions and the image of a lion on the top (the Buddha was often referred to as the Lion of the Shakyas). His son, Malinda, took the faith to Ceylon (present day Sri Lanka) where its main scriptures were recorded in the Pali Canon (the Tipitaka) around the first century BCE. There is thus a period of around 400 years when the Buddha's Teachings were preserved by oral tradition and memorization. The powers of the human brain for memorization are formidable and were commonly used by early people who would often divide the load between different individuals in a monastery and chant the teachings in a verse form which was easier to remember. We must recall that in Judaism there was an interval of approximately eight centuries before the acts and utterances of Moses were set down in formal writings. In the case of Christianity there was an interval of at least forty years between Christ's teachings and its recording in the Gospel of

Mark. In Islam, the holy book of the Koran is felt to have been compiled approximately twenty years after the death of Mohamed. From this nucleus Buddhism eventually spread into Southeast Asia (mainly in the Therevada form) and into the orient (in the Mahayana form). The number of Buddhists in the world in estimated to be approximately one thousand million.

Variants of Buddhism

From the stimulus of the Buddha's life and teachings, a variety of forms of Buddhism have arisen due to human contemplation and inventiveness—these are factors in the development of any great religion. These are as follows.

Theravada.

This has been termed "the way of the elders" as it probably embraces most of the factors of the earliest Buddhism. This is found in the countries of Southeast Asia namely Burma (Myanmar), Cambodia, Laos, and Thailand. It comprises the following features:

- A way for the Individual. It has been termed the Individual Way.
- The Centrality of the Individual termed the Arahant and his or her personal salvation.
- Nirvana as the object of the Individual's efforts. This is most certainly achieved in a monastic setting but it may also be sought by the lay individual although it may require a much longer period and indeed several lives to achieve it.
- The object is to transcend the Wheel of Life (Samsara).

It is sometimes known as the "Minor vehicle," although some of its followers have felt that this is pejorative.

Mahayana.

This form has been practiced in China, Tibet, Mongolia, Nepal, Korea, and Japan. It dates probably from the first century BCE when it arose in Northern India. It has the following features:

- A Universal Way for all persons.
- The Concept of the Bodhisattva. Instead of the faith being concerned with the salvation of the individual, the Bodhisattva is someone who could achieve salvation in the form of Nirvana but seeks not to do so until they have used all their efforts to achieve the salvation of all other sentient beings. Sentient beings are the human species but also

all of the animal world and may even extend into the plant world. The most celebrated Bodhisattva is the mythical Avalokiteshvara who is an embodiment of Compassion itself.

• The realization that Samsara is itself Nirvana. In other words we can find our salvation not on some far shore but in and amongst the turmoil of daily life. This requires us to achieve Equanimity and to blend our concept of self with those others around us, which is indeed a challenging task involving benevolence and compassion.

• Buddha Bhakti. Although the Buddha is recorded as denying that he was a god or even a diva, his image starts to be revered. There is indeed the concept of multiple Buddha's or Enlightened Ones in the four quarters of the universe.

• Trikaya. Here there is a concept of multiple tiers of Enlightened Ones, namely:

    a. Earthly Enlightened Ones, Nirmanakaya: The Buddha, Siddhartha Gautama, is the prime figure here.

    b. Transcendent Heavenly Enlightened Ones: Sambhogakaya. These are heavenly Buddha's such as Amida Buddha, felt in Pure Land Buddhism to reside in the Western Paradise.

    c. Cosmic Enlightenment: Dharmakaya. This relates to a non-anthropomorphic image of the way or Dharma. It equates with the abstract mystical concept of the God Head in other religions such as Nirguna Brahman in Hinduism, En Soph in Judaism, the Logos in Christianity, Al Haq in Islam and the Eternal Tao in Taoism.

The Relevance of Buddhism in Today's World of Suffering.

Why have I chosen to give so much space to Buddhism? The proliferation of Buddhism throughout the world and the development of Buddhist ideas is a significant event. Indeed, one may be put off by the many exotic proliferations that have occurred—discussion of Zen and Tantra, fascinating though these are in the study of the development of religion, has been omitted for the sake of balance. We may however summarize the relevance of Buddhism in our present search under the following headings:

• It provides a Philosopher Archetype for religion.

• It extols Compassion which is the Golden Rule of all religions.

• It emphasizes Mindfulness. Surely the only way to the solution of the world's problems is for the human mind to be active and resourceful?

• It centralizes the importance of the Truth.

- It has a Cosmic Viewpoint.
- It has an inspired and charming iconography.

THE LINKS BETWEEN SOCRATES AND BUDDHA: IMPERTURBABILITY

These two men were individualist thinkers of the Axial Age. They both provided a rethinking of the concept of the ancient Gods. They both were convinced of the central importance of Mind. Socrates brought out the mind by the Discursive, Dialectical Method. The Buddha plumbed the mind by Introspection and Meditation. Both men were concerned with a search for true inner happiness as opposed to a superficial content. Socrates was concerned to explore the sensual basis for this (Eros). The Buddha sought the attainment of Bliss (Nirvana). Both men exemplified the quality of Imperturbability or Equanimity amongst the chaos of their own world, which has application to the continuing chaos of our own modern world. We will draw on a number of much more modern philosophers, particularly those with a religious concern, as we progress but these two iconic figures have an enduring quality.

Answer: These two complimentary schools of thought, one Western and one Eastern, point to meaning in the Examined Life and in a pragmatic Path—both conceived in the fruitful Axial Period.

Reading List and Sources
An Introduction to Greek Philosophy. J. V. Luce, Thames and Hudson.1992.
Buddha. Karen Armstrong. Weidenfeld and Nicolson.2002.

CHAPTER 3. THE ATHEISTS

Sigmund Freud and Richard Dawkins

Question: Is belief in a Creator Deity of the Abrahamic
tradition a hindrance to an honest search for Meaning or does
its denial remove the essence of all ultimate significance?

Agnosticism and Atheism can themselves be seen as default positions in
an Existentialist and Post Modern situation. However, they are also ancient
in the pattern of man's thought and one is mindful of the Sophists in ancient
Greece who pronounced everything ultimately meaningless. Let us note the
following saying about Agnosticism: "An Agnostic is a cowardly Atheist"
(Studs Terkel, 2003).

This brings a smile to the lips but is rather unfair. The Agnostic is uncertain and may well ask for further evidence before he or she makes up
their mind. I think that this is a very reasonable position and one that one
should respect. It will epitomize this position in chapter six when we talk
about Charles Darwin. On the other hand, there is something rather bleak
about Atheism illustrated in the following anonymous epitaph: "Here lies
an Atheist, all dressed up with nowhere to go."

SIGMUND FREUD

Again, one respects the Atheist viewpoint but shivers a little as in a cold
wind at the realization of all its implications. We feel ourselves as a naked
ape confined within a sometimes very hostile world which has no higher
meaning. Let us examine the life of one eminent exponent of this viewpoint,
namely Sigmund Freud.

Life Details of Sigmund Freud

He was born in Moravia to Jewish parents, but spent most of his life in Vienna until he was persuaded reluctantly to leave in 1938 when Hitler took over Austria. He moved to England and the USA, in exile, only to die in the following year under sad circumstances.

He was a neurologist known for his initiation of psychoanalysis and his development of the concept of the subconscious mind. He had studied for a period under Charcot in Paris and later with Breuer. His early books were *Studies of Hysteria* (1895) and *Interpretation of Dreams* (1900). Freud regarded the subconscious mind as a repository for repressed feelings whose content was often too unpleasant for the conscious mind to face up to. It was in a way the trash box of the mind, whose contents would continually surface to the discomfort of the individual who was not aware of the origins of his neurosis—although this could be revealed for him by psychoanalysis. This was in opposition to the views of his contemporary associate Carl Jung, leading to their eventual stormy parting. Jung regarded the unconscious mind as more of a treasure house rather than a trash box, particularly as it contained, in his view, the collective unconscious, conceived as a sort of archive of the species' symbolic images which might surface in dreams and religious practices.

Freud's Views on Religion

Freud came from a Jewish background but was himself an Atheist. He was preoccupied with the underlying psychology of religion. He gave much thought to the role of Moses as the founder figure of Judaism related in his monograph *Moses and Monotheism*. He regarded the figure of Jehovah as portrayed in the Old Testament as a very savage one as for example in his exhortation to Moses to pillage Canaan in the entry of the Jews into the Promised Land. He felt that Moses had derived this image of a sort of Volcano God from his wife who was the daughter of a Midianite Priest— the Midianites worshiped a volcano God called Jave, according to Freud. I had the good fortune to visit Freud's old Consulting Room in Vienna. There one saw photographs of the collection of symbolic figures from many of the world religions which he placed on his desk as a sort of reference archive.

Freud expressed his Atheist viewpoint, derived from his study of World Religions, in two seminal books. The first was entitled *Totem and Taboo*. This was initial data in which he explored the psychological mechanisms behind the use of totem animals in primal communities and religious taboos or forbidden areas such as incest. It was however, in his next book, entitled *The Future of an Illusion* that the very title indicates his views on the nature of religious belief. He felt, on psychological grounds that the God Image was a projection of the Father Image. He suggested a scenario in the far past in which the young men killed the Father to appropriate his female cohorts and his goods. The sons were later to be overcome with remorse so that they sanctified the image of the old man in the form of ancestor worship. Not only did Freud regard religion as illusory, but it was also pernicious in that it led to neurosis due to its unreasonable concentration on feelings of guilt. In fact, he regarded religion as "a generalized neurosis." These were honestly held views and one respects them. However one suspects that they tore Freud apart as a person in that he could never forget his Jewish origins. In his consulting room, I saw a bust fashioned not too long before his death and one sensed the immense sadness expressed on his face.

Freud's Final Years

Freud became increasingly an isolationist in his relationships with others. At the end he came to regard the company of his two dogs as superior to that of his fellow human beings. One is mindful of his predecessor philosopher Schopenhauer; whose mordant semi-Buddhist philosophy had an effect on Freud's own views. Schopenhauer came to prefer the company of his poodle over his human compatriots! Freud sadly suffered over the later years of his life from a malignant tumor of the upper jaw which required repeated operations and his wearing an occlusive form of denture known as an obturator (Freud used to call it "the monster"). Ernest Jones, his biographer, chronicled the sad events of his final days. The malignant tumor came to fungate through Freud's cheek permeating a terrible, nauseating odor. The dogs could not stand this and slunk away from his company. This was a final great sadness for Freud, and one can empathize with his feelings.

Assessment

Freud holds and deserves a special place in the history of psychology and indeed the psychology of religion. Much of his work is now regarded as intuitive rather than scientific particularly regarding to the proven efficacy of psychoanalysis and his preoccupation with sex and the Oedipus complex. His views were honestly held and one respects that he suffered for them and with them. Nobody can doubt that projection has played a major role in the development in an anthropomorphic image of the Intelligence behind life. Xenophanes would have given a wry smile had he been around at that time!

RICHARD DAWKINS

Richard Dawkins is almost certainly the best known modern exponent of atheism being the author of a controversial new book *The God Delusion* published in 2006. Interestingly, the book has a shiny silver dust jacket so that when one looks straight at the word God one sees a reflection of one's own face! This appeared to me to be very Freudian in view of Freud's suggestion that the Deity is merely a projection of the human image. Strangely, Dawkins does not mention Freud and maybe this is because he is embarrassed by an image of pseudo science. I heard Dawkins lecture in the august surroundings of the Royal Society about twenty five years ago but still remember the occasion vividly. His degree of conviction and attack were impressive but I found his determined reductionism rather too abrasive for my own mind-set at that stage. He narrated that he had designed a computer program for his young daughter so that she could create a series of human like forms which he called "biomorphs." By this means, she would be able to mimic human evolution in that it was a simple process as outlined by Charles Darwin. Darwin indicated three basic processes namely:

- A process of Common Descent.
- Natural Selection.
- Random Mutation.

Dawkins is the foremost proponent of Neo Darwinism. Darwin did not know about the existence of genes and DNA. Neo Darwinism takes the whole process from there and develops it into an intricately coordinated explanation of the evolution of life without the role of a Creator or Intelligent Design. Paradoxically, Dawkins has had the greatest difficulty in fitting the concept of God easily into the scheme of Darwinian Evolution!

Dawkin's Career

Dawkins was born in 1941 in Nairobi in Kenya as the son of a farmer and former soldier. It was a distinguished family mentioned in Burke's Landed Gentry. He had a conventional religious background in the Anglican tradition. At the age of eight his parents moved to England and he was educated at the elitist Oundle School. It was at the age of about sixteen years that he learned about the theory of evolution which meant that he no longer needed a concept of a designer behind life. He studied Zoology at Balliol College, Oxford gaining eventually the post graduate degrees of MA and PhD and eventually DSc. His tutor at Oxford was the Nobel Prize Laureate Nikolas Tinbergen. Tinbergen was an eminent Danish Biologist who was the author of the book *The Study of Instinct* which was a celebrated work on animal behavior. The study of animal behavior has been termed Ethology. The concepts of Ethology have influenced Dawkins in his subsequent work and publications. Dawkins was an assistant professor of zoology at the University of California, Berkeley from 1967 to 1969. Subsequently he was appointed a lecturer in zoology at the University of Oxford in 1970 going on to become a reader in 1990. A specially endowed professor's post was created for him by the philanthropist Charles Simony in 1995 being entitled Professor for the Public Understanding of Science. Simony entitled Dawkins as "Darwin's Rottweiler" in the tradition of Thomas Huxley who had in earlier years been entitled "Darwin's bulldog"! Dawkins has always been a very controversial figure but has acquired many honors including Fellowship of the Royal Society in 2001; this is an accolade for any scientist in the United Kingdom.

Dawkins's Books

Dawkins has produced twelve widely-read books including the *The God Delusion*. The most celebrated of these are:

- *The Selfish Gene* (1976).

Here he proposes an ethology of the gene which he describes as a replicator. He states: "All life evolves by the differential survival of replicating entities." (Dawkins 1976)

This has been described as producing a conceptual bridge between the reductionist imperatives of molecular biology and the taxonomies of zoology, psychology, and sociology.

- *The Extended Phenotype* (1982).

Here he describes natural selection as "The process whereby replicators out-propagate each other." (Dawkins 1982)

The extended phenotype propagates itself beyond the individual to take in the family of the organism, its social group and the whole of its environment to its own selfish advantage. He raises the disturbing question of whether human DNA actually controls the technosphere of our life and surroundings in an almost automaton context.

- *The Blind Watchmaker* (1986).

Here is presented the criticism of the argument from design as an evidence for the existence of God. The title is a reference to the renowned Victorian book *Natural Theology*, by the Reverend William Paley, where he sees God as a Divine Watchmaker who sets the mechanism of the World in motion; this is the Deist philosophy whereby the Creator is like Aristotle's Unmoved Mover who initiates the world but takes no further active part in its running. Dawkins feels that the theory of evolution makes this teleological argument unnecessary; there is no need for the concept of a designer in the scheme.

Dawkins' other works are: *River Out of Eden* (1995), *Climbing Mount Improbable* (1996), *Unweaving the Rainbow* (1998), *A Devil's Chaplain* (2003), *The Ancestor's Tale* (2004)—in all of these he develops his theories on Neo Darwinism and evolution. His latest book is *The Greatest Show On Earth* (2009} where he summarizes his justification for Evolution versus Creationism-we will critique it in Chapter 6.

Dawkins's View on Religion

Dawkins's is characteristically uncompromising regarding the concept of a personal omnipotent God as a delusion which he defines as a "false belief or impression." He quotes the author Robert Pirsig as saying: "When one person suffers from a delusion, it is called insanity. When many people suffer from a delusion it is called Religion" (Pirsig, 1981).

This is very reminiscent of Freud's description of religion as a "a generalized neurosis." He explains that he has no quarrel with the use of the term God as a metaphor by certain eminent scientists and philosophers in the categories:

• Pantheism.

The Philosopher Spinoza saw god not in anthropomorphic form but as equating with the world and nature itself.

• Deism.

Such thinkers as Voltaire, Diderot, and more recently Einstein have espoused this concept of God as an underlying phenomenon behind life but not intimately involved with it.

• A Mixture of Pantheism and Deism.

He cites Paul Davies, the physicist, as an example of this attitude.

Otherwise, he is merciless in his critique of the God of the Old Testament: "The God of the Old Testament is arguably the most unpleasant character in all fiction; jealous and proud of it; a petty unjust, unforgiving control-freak; a vindictive, blood thirsty ethnic cleanser; a misogynistic, homophobic, racist, infanticidal, genocidal, filicidal, pestilential, megalo-maniacal, sadomasochistic, capriciously malevolent bully" (Dawkins 2006).

Wow! After this devastating attack, he gives several examples of what he calls Jahweh's "deplorable character":

- In Genesis, God is displeased with the whole human race so he sets out to destroy them all and most of the animal world in a devastating Flood. That is all except for Noah and his family and a small selection of animal life. This is a very vindictive action with apparently a minimal justification.

- The destruction of the cities of Sodom and Gomorrah for rather uncertain unnatural practices.

- God ordered Abraham to sacrifice his only son Isaac only reversing his decision at the last moment which must have caused great distress to both father and child.

- On Mount Sinai, Moses was constrained because of God's jealousy to order the priestly tribe of Levi to kill by the sword as many as possible of those who had been involved in the worship of the Golden Calf-this was around three thousand persons.

- In the book of Numbers, God incited Moses to attack the Midi-anites, burn their cities and kill all men and women except the young virgins.

- God's savage instructions for the invasion of The Promised Land: "But of the cities of these people, which the Lord Thy God thus gave thee for an inheritance, thou shall save alive nothing that breathes: But thou shall utterly destroy them; namely, the Hittites, and the Amorites, the Canaanites, and the Perizzites, the Hivites and the Jubisites; as the Lord Thy God hath commanded thee" (Bible: Deuteronomy 20:16, 17).

Dawkins gives himself some support for this attack by a quotation from Thomas Jefferson: "The Christian God is a being of terrific character—cruel, vindictive, capricious and unjust" (Dawkins, 2006).

Dawkins extends his caustic comments to the Bible, which he consid-ers is: "...just plain weird, as you would expect of a chaotically coupled-to-gether anthology of disjointed documents, composed, revised, translated, distorted, and 'improved' by hundreds of anonymous authors, editors, and copyists, unknown to us and mostly unknown to each other, spanning nine centuries" (Dawkins, 2006).

Dawkins does not extend his criticism to the figure of Allah and the book of the Koran although he is very outspoken about the events of September 11 and the misguided views of anyone involved in terrorism and self sacrifice who feel they will be rewarded by their God. He undoubtedly had in mind the fate of Salman Rushdie after the publication of his book *The Satanic Verses*, who faced a fatwa in the form of a death threat; Dawkins was one of a group of writers who spoke in his defense. Dawkins's reaction after the September 11, 2001, attacks is that prior to this many saw religion as "harmless nonsense" but that has changed.

> Beliefs might lack all supporting evidence but, we thought, if people needed a crutch for consolation where's the harm? September the eleventh changed all that. Revealed faith is not harmless nonsense; it can be lethally dangerous nonsense. Dangerous because it gives people unshakeable confidence in their own righteousness. Dangerous because it gives them false courage to kill themselves, which automatically removes normal barriers to killing others. Dangerous because it teaches enmity to others labeled only by a difference of inherited tradition. (Dawkins, 2006)

He comments that it is also dangerous because we have all bought into a "weird" respect, which uniquely protects religion from normal criticism. Dawkins sums up by commenting that we should stop being so "damned" respectful! These are fighting words which take a lot of courage to utter.

THE EVOLUTION OF RELIGION

There are a number of theories on the evolution of religion as a human activity:

1. Adaptive (David Sloan Wilson).

Here the presence of a religion is felt to give social cohesion to a human group and help it to survive in the process of natural selection. (Sloan Wilson 2007)

2. A Byproduct (Pascal Boyer).

Here religion is seen as an accidental byproduct of other adaptive processes. (Pascal Boyer 2001)

3. A Spandrel (Stephen Jay Gould).

The eminent biologist the late Stephen Jay Gould propounded this theory. A spandrel is the incidental but nonfunctional structure between arches in a building. This is really a variant of the byproduct theory. (Jay Gould 1999)

4. A Cultural Meme.

This was the theory that Dawkins favored. He could not think that religion was a favorable adaptive mechanism in the process of genetic natural selection. It was after all a delusion and as such wasteful of time and effort that would be better devoted to food gathering, procreation, and defense. Dawkins coined the term "meme" in *The Selfish Gene*. A meme is defined in the Oxford English Dictionary as "An element of culture that may be considered to be passed on by non-genetic means."

For once, Dawkins seems to stumble somewhat and needs to struggle to explain why religion should have survived so well and so long. Daniel Dennett in his 2006 book *Breaking the Spell: Religion as a Natural Phenomenon* is another noted atheist. He is Professor of Philosophy at Tufts University. He is much more sympathetic for the comforting and supporting role of religion in the world and expresses concern for the vacuum that its loss will provide in a suffering world. We will discuss his book later.

Freud And Dawkins

I think that Freud would have approved of Dawkin's uncompromising attitude to religion even though Dawkins himself seems reluctant to be labeled as a Freudian! It takes a lot of courage to express such opinions. Freud undoubtedly paid the penalties for this and ended a sad man. Dawkins has tremendous bounce and is living in a very different more tolerant era. Darwin himself had to exercise caution in his religious doubts because he had great respect for his loving wife who was very conventional in her religious attitudes. One notes, that Dawkins has been married three times. He is currently married to the actress and artist Lalla Ward. They obviously have a fellow feeling for his sentiments in that she has illustrated two of his books, *River Out of Eden* and *Climbing Mount Improbable*. One needs a kindred spirit in such enterprises!

Answer: There is a fear that discarding a belief in the anthropomorphic image of the God of the Abrahamic tradition will deprive us of an ethical code to give meaning to life, but it is relevant to remember that such a code is present in the six great non-theistic faiths of the world and indeed in humanism, as we will discuss later.

Reading List and Sources
Life and Work of Sigmund Freud. Ernest Jones, Penguin Books. 1993.

The God Delusion. Richard Dawkins. Houghton Mifflin Company. Bantam Press 2006.

CHAPTER 4. SENSUALISTS IN THE CAUSE OF ART

Paul Gauguin and Vincent Van Gogh

Question: The Senses can undoubtedly bring
us a form of bliss either through Art or Sexuality but
is it too short lived to give true meaning?

THE ROLE OF ART: LIVING THROUGH THE SENSES

The species *Homo Sapiens* will produce at least four types of instinctual activity namely language, religion, visual arts, and music. In each of these endeavors there is a tremendous variety of expression, which can be attributed to man's inventiveness. Cave painting came into prominence in the Upper Paleolithic Age. The first European sites that were discovered were in Altamira in Northern Spain and are felt to date to approximately 15 thousand years ago (although there are other sites still older). I have been fortunate enough to visit the Altamira caves, although they are not open to the general public, due to the influence of my Spanish wife, Carmen, and a little gentle Spanish nepotism! At first, no one would agree that these momentous artifacts were the work of so called primitive people, although this is now established. I will never forget the impact of going deep into the hillside, amongst stalagmites, and stalactites, to suddenly come upon startlingly vivid representations of the animals of that period, ranging from the delicacy of a deer to the might of an enraged bison, glowing under the lights within the chasm itself. What was the impetus to produce such representations in dark, inhospitable locations within the bowels of the earth? It was first felt to relate to hunting magic, but now there is wide acclaim for the view that it relates to Shamanic religion. The Shaman is the earliest religious figure—he is a spirit of nature and ecstasy. In some of the other caves, he is depicted as half man and half animal (as in Les Trois Frères cave in France), providing a bridge between man and the natural world. So from their first inception, works of visual art have had a numinous quality to them.

The Views of the Philosopher Schopenhauer on Art

The German philosopher Arthur Schopenhauer (1788-1860) was preoccupied with the existence of human suffering, so that he has sometimes been called "the philosopher of pessimism," although his main emphasis was to suggest ways of escaping from that suffering in an eastern Buddhist style. His major work was entitled *The World as Will and Idea*. He termed the fundamental power which moves and underlies all things the Will to Live. The philosopher Adler termed this all pervading force the Will to Power. The Will manifests itself in a miserable, perpetual struggle in which all beings suffer and fight mercilessly for their very existence. The world is a place of restless desire and ruthless egoistic striving, devoid of any real personal freedom, ruled by the overwhelming determination of the Will. The Will has been implanted into all living beings as a manifestation of a Universal Will, which is totally unrelenting in its demands. There are however four main ways, according to Schopenhauer, by which the individual may seek to escape the harsh calls of the Will:

Through exercising the fellow instinct of compassion

Learning to practice a total denial of the will

Through a contemplation of the Platonic Forms, those eternal templates which Plato visualized as behind our mortal lives, epitomized by such entities as the good, beauty and truth.

The genuine artist will present the Platonic Forms as underlying universals behind life. This makes possible a spiritual liberation through Art whereby the noisy ego is silenced, and we can be freed from possessive, selfish desires and anxieties.

This escape from the turmoil of our normal frenetic activity is at the risk of reducing our view of the normal external world to a sort of Nothingness, similar to the vision of the existentialists such as Sartre, who was influenced by Schopenhauer's concepts. Schopenhauer himself likened it to lifting of the veil of Maya, an eastern image of the illusion that is presented by the superficial external aspects of our human life. Schopenhauer felt that all the arts were valuable in this aspect including the visual art of painting: "In music and arts we can contemplate the universal Will apart from our own individual strivings." (Schopenhauer, 1818)

Heidegger, another existentialist philosopher who came under Schopenhauer's potent influence, mentioned the specific images of Van Gogh's chair and Van Gogh's peasant's shoes as visual images that present a universal aspect in their impact.

The Universal Will is eternal and our individual lives are not to be valued since it is the Will's desire to exist in the world of appearances that gives rise to our individual existence and consequently our suffering. The arts involve a special emphasis on the senses of sight and hearing, Schopenhauer however cautioned that the Will to Expression for the artist can be as all consuming and dangerous as is the Will to Power of the politician or militarist.

We wish to examine that will in the case of two artists who both paid a harsh ultimate price for their unique works of art, which they gave to our world helping us towards our own freedom in Schopenhauer's sense. Their two lives came together at one point in a devastating conflagration, which shook both of them to the core. Let us examine their lives as Sensualists.

THE PASSIONATE LIFE EVENTS OF PAUL GAUGUIN (1848–1903)

He was born in Paris but spent his early childhood in Lima, Peru. He was the grandson of Flora Tristan, a founder of modern feminism from whom he may have acquired some of his spirit of non conformity. His schooling was in Orleans in France. Following this, he spent six years of his life sailing around the world, first in merchant ships, and then in the French navy. This obviously gave him his spirit of restlessness and desire for far flung shores, as his later life exemplified. He managed to settle down into the respectable life of a stock broker working on the Paris Stock Exchange, and was initially very successful. He was a talented amateur painter in his spare time and was introduced to Camille Pissarro, whose benign influence on young painters gave him the title of "Father of Impressionism." The School of Impressionism, exemplified by such artists as Monet, Renoir, and Degas had a huge liberating effect on the visual arts. It freed academic art from a tired adherence to Form. Impressionists brought in a concern for color, vibration, and life. Unfortunately, in 1882 the French stock market collapsed and many employees were laid off, including Gauguin. Whether this was the real reason why Gauguin abandoned his profession or whether it was an excuse to allow him expression of his developing passion for painting and his wanderlust is debatable. One suspects the latter; but in any case, he sent his wife with their five children to her parents in Denmark and devoted the rest of his life to a restless and passionate abandonment to his muse. He sought out far flung parts of the world seeking primitive environments which would satisfy his desire for exoticism. His journeys took him to Martinique, Tahiti, and the Marquesas. It was his practice in the two latter locations to seek out a female in her early teens (a Vahini) to live with him, as a paid companion, despite the lack of any language in common save that of physical love. This earned him the condemnation of the local Catholic missionaries. The Vahinis had the compensation for what must have been a tumultuous and disturbing relationship by being immortalized in his paintings. Gauguin's bold experimentation with coloring was appropriate to tropical environments in which he found himself and led directly to the synthetist style of modern art. He used a cloisonnistic style of outlining areas of pure color which is credited for paving the way to Primitivism and a return to the pastoral. He was plagued by lack of funding and recurrent illness, dying in his eccentric dwelling known as "House of Pleasure" on the island of Hiva Oa. Over the lintel of that house was inscribed a motto for his way of life: "Be Mysterious and Be In Love and You Will Be Happy" (Gauguin, "House of Pleasure").

Before he died, he painted a huge work directly onto sackcloth entitled "Where Do We Come From? What Are We? Where Are We Going?" These are the great questions behind all life in images of birth, death, and sensuality, and Pagan religion, brilliantly evoked in a welter of tropical, exotic coloration and form. It is undoubtedly one of the greatest works of art of the world, and is currently housed in the Museum of Modern Art in Boston. Its creator was to die prematurely at the age of 55, apparently of the effects of syphilis (the disease of indiscriminate love) penniless, alone, and embittered; such is the irony of life!

THE TORMENTED LIFE EVENTS OF VINCENT VAN GOGH (1853–1890)

Van Gogh was a contemporary of Gauguin having been born five years after him in Holland, the son of an impoverished Calvinist preacher. He in-

herited a religious outlook from his father unlike Gauguin's listless sensualism. He had to finish his studies at the age of fifteen due to his family's
circumstances. He joined an art dealer's firm which occupation took him
to The Hague in Holland, London, and Paris. However he had a passionate
desire to serve God. He longed to undertake the vocation of either a pastor
or missionary but this was to be cruelly denied to him in that he was refused
admittance, on the grounds of failing the examination, to the Theological
Faculty of Amsterdam and was rapidly rejected as a novitiate of a modest
theological school at Lacken, near Brussels. In desperation, he took himself
to the area of coal mining in the Borinage in Belgium where he wanted to be
a poor man amongst the poor. Without reward all day long, he visited the
sick and preached the Gospel to the miners. He earned his keep by giving
lessons to the salesmen's children in the evenings. He started to produce
brilliant drawings portraying the overwhelming misery of the miners that
he saw everyday around him. These were somber dark creations already
demonstrating the artist's talent for expressionism. After an unrequited
and inappropriate love affair, he made an even more outlandish relationship
with a thirty-two-year old prostitute who was pregnant, an alcoholic, and
who suffered from syphilis. She had a five-year-old daughter. He had come
to know her "from need of vital warmth and health reasons." Sien was her
nickname, and Vincent immortalized her in such drawings as "Sorrow," in
1882, where she is portrayed as a female nude in a pose of total desperation,
with sagging breasts and distorted abdomen. With typical passion and unrealistic self sacrifice, Vincent desperately wanted to marry her in order to
save her. He was only dissuaded from this by her constant unfaithfulness
and the coercion of his family.

In all of this, Vincent's constant confidant was his brother Theo. Their
correspondence in letters over the whole period of their inter woven lives is
a classic example of mutual devotion Schopenhauer advocated compassion
as one way out of life's willful battle and Theo exemplified this great virtue
in all his dealings with his brother. He supported him morally and also with
whatever finance he could spare. Vincent had a strange, borderline personality, probably due to a combination of bi-polar disorder and epilepsy. He
now realized that his life's mission could no longer relate to the Church but
must be with a career in painting. Theo helped him as always in the provi-
sion of materials and tuition. Vincent methodically increased his repertoire
from drawing through figure representation into the introduction of color.

At first his palette was somber and muted, as in his painting "The Potato Eaters" of 1885 in which he portrays a family of peasants sitting down in a tiny dark cottage around a humble meal of potatoes. He stated: "I have tried to emphasize that these people, eating their potatoes in the lamplight, have dug the earth with those same hands that they put in the dish, and so it speaks of manual labor and how they have honestly earned their food" (Van Gogh, 1885).

Contact with Impressionism

In 1886 Vincent took himself to Paris for two reasons; he was convinced that living there with his brother Theo, he would be able to save money and he wanted to join the studio of a painter known as Corman. At the studio, he met fellow students like Emile Bernard and Henri de Toulouse-Lautrec, and what is more important he became aware of the great Impressionist movement that was in full sway in Paris at that time. It was an event of huge moment for him. His style enlarged enormously in its scope and his palette opened up to include vibrant hues. He met most of the Impressionist painters who are now household names, and in particular encountered and set out to befriend Paul Gauguin who had just arrived in Paris.

Eventually he felt worn out from the life in Paris despite its stimulation and indeed he had painted over 200 works during his two years there. He decided to leave to go to Arles in Provence. He signed a lease to rent four rooms in the "yellow house" in the Place du Forum. The clear light of Provence permeated his whole style and increased his passion. I am an amateur painter myself, but in the rather somber light of England I was always concerned about my lack of drive. It was only when I visited the South of France, in Provence itself, that the vibrant light motivated me to paint in oils in a way I had never previously experienced. The same southern sunshine motivated Vincent to use primary colors (reds, yellows, and blues) which were squeezed straight from the tube onto the canvas and were spread with direct, broad, sweeping brushstrokes. Everything was grist to his mill, particularly landscapes, café scenes, self portraits, night scenes and above all his most celebrated subject of sunflowers. Sunflowers seem to epitomize his fascination with nature and it is believed he had painted twelve different versions in all.

The Agony of Loneliness

Vincent was however lonely and desperately wanted other painters to share with him his view on painting and his preoccupation with the brilliant sunshine of the South of France. On the 23rd of October of 1888 Gauguin arrived in Arles after repeated requests from Van Gogh. This tumultuous short lived relationship set off a terrible chain of events which led to the breakdown of Vincent's fragile mental life. Vincent had so hoped that the two painters could inter-relate and co-operate but Gauguin found that Vincent's behavior verged on madness. Their stormy inter-relationship will be documented shortly. After a resulting violent fit of delirium, Vincent needed to be admitted to the Hotel-Dieu Hospital in Arles where he was locked up in a cell. Later he had to be taken to the asylum of Saint-Paul-de-Mausole near Saint-Remy-de-Provence. Despite his illness, Vincent would still paint in the interior of his hospital and asylum poignant tortured images. He even painted his doctors, particularly Dr Gachet, an enigmatic physician who was a painter himself and a friend of several Impressionists. Vincent did not have absolute confidence in the doctor, however, and indeed he was unable to substantially help his increasingly disturbed patient. Events were rapidly coming to a tragic conclusion. Shortly before this, Vincent's painting "Wheat Field under Threatening Skies with Crows" was painted. The black outlines of the crows are seen over a violently spatulated panorama of cornfields under a dark blue lowering sky, betokening a terrible hidden menace.

Vincent's despair was deepened still further by the information by his brother that he would no longer be able to carry on with his financial support because his wife was expecting a baby. On July 27, 1890, at the age of 37, he walked disconsolately into the fields and shot himself with a revolver. He died two days later, with Theo by his side, who reported his last words as, "Sadness will last forever" (Van Gogh in Pascal Bonafoux 1992). Six months later Theo himself was to die prematurely from the effects, apparently, of grief and syphilis. Vincent and Theo's graves lie side by side at the cemetery of Auvers-sur-Oise.

Out of a prodigious production of some 800 paintings, Vincent in his entire lifetime had only sold one canvas. His works might well have been lost to the world if it hadn't been for the efforts of his sister-in-law and the benevolent Père Tanguy, the friend of so many painters in need, who stored his paintings in Paris. On March 30, 1987, Christie's, the celebrated art dealers in London, auctioned one of Van Gogh's "Sunflowers" for the world record price of about £25 million. Such is the irony of life!

The Stormy Events in the Relationship between Gauguin and Van Gogh in Arles 1888

Let us backtrack. For two months these two men lived together in the Yellow House, exhibiting one of the most tempestuous and extraordinary relationships of all time. Vincent desperately needed a companion and a master but it was beyond Gauguin's abilities and patience to satisfy him. Vincent had gone to great lengths to furnish the house having bought two beds (one made of walnut, one made of white wood), two mattresses, 12 chairs and a mirror. It was described that he gave the house a "Daumier-like character." He always thought of things and events in relationship to his knowledge of the great painters. Although his own room had all the characteristics of an austere monastic cell, he had decorated Gauguin's room with pictures of sunflowers as "like the boudoir of a really artistic woman." Gauguin got off the train at dawn at Arles and was met by Ginoux, Vincent's friend who owned the Café de Lagare. He recognized Gauguin from a self-portrait that he had seen.

The two men's temperaments were very different; Vincent was initially nervous and deferential whereas Gauguin was confident and somewhat overbearing. Gauguin characteristically quickly started to organize their life. He did the cooking and organized their joint preparation of canvases and stretchers. Vincent commented, "With Gauguin, blood and sex triumph over ambition" (Van Gogh in Pascal Bonafoux 1992).

Gauguin organized their scanty resources, apportioning their money for their various needs, including visits to the local brothels "for hygienic purposes." In the first month, they worked together, talking and preparing ideas. Gauguin painted Vincent painting sunflowers. Van Gogh saw the painting and commented, "It's me alright, but it's me gone mad!" (Van Gogh in Pascal Bonafoux 1992)

In the second month, however, an uneasy equilibrium was set up. Instead of conversations, there were confrontations with, according to Vincent, "excessive electricity." Gauguin became restless and wanted to leave Arles. Vincent was distraught and could not believe this, fearing a return to solitude. On December 23, 1888, escaping from the tense atmosphere, Gauguin took a walk on his own after dinner in the town. He became aware of footsteps behind him and turned around to see Vincent bearing down on him, brandishing an open razor. He then appeared to change his mind and returned to the Yellow House. Gauguin, not unnaturally, made the decision to go to a hotel for the night. He came back to the Yellow House next day to find that there was a crowd outside together with policemen. He was told that Vincent appeared to be dead. The house was full of bloodstained towels, and there were blood spatters on the walls and staircase. Vincent was lying in his bed, unconscious. It appeared that he had cut off part of his ear and then gone to a local brothel at 11:30pm asking for one of the girls, Rachel. He handed her the part of his ear, saying, "keep this object carefully." Gauguin did what he could to help. He asked that a doctor be summoned and then sent a telegram to Theo in Paris before leaving himself by train for that city. He was filled with resolve to leave the influence of civilization and started to make his arrangements to travel to Tahiti. In an interview he stated: "I need to renew myself in unspoiled nature, to see nothing but savages, to live as they do, with no other concern but to convey as a child might, what my mind conceives, abetted only by primitive means of expression, the only right and true ones there are." (Gauguin 1891)

Vincent commented in a letter to Theo, "But as for him... Lord, let him do anything he wants, let him have his independence? (whatever he means by that) and his opinions...." (Van Gogh 1889)

Thereby ended one of the strangest and most eventful exchanges in the history of art. From there, Vincent entered into the sad sequence of developing mental breakdown previously chronicled.

Meaning in Sexuality

I have delayed writing this section until all else has been completed, hesitating to come to conclusions on this all important topic. For most of us sexual communion will provide an experience of sensual bliss beyond anything else that we have ever experienced. Its power in directing our actions cannot be overestimated. It inspires poets at one extreme and ruins lives from its injudicious pursuit at the other. Wherein lies its meaning?—is it an example of divine providence or a malicious snare for the unwary? Both our artists were vulnerable to its dictates as in Vincent's unrealistic passion for Sian and Paul's unrepentant use of vahinis. Both men were constrained to visit brothels "for hygienic purposes." Their vibrant use of color could be seen as a manifestation of their passionate libidos.

D.H. Lawrence chastened the western world when his sexually explicit novel *Lady Chatterley's Lover* was first published in Italy in 1928—it could not appear in Great Britain until 1960 after it was tested in an historic court case under the Obscene Publications Act. Its chief character Connie (Lady Chatterley) finds the potency of her true sexuality in her irregular relationship with Mellors, her husband's gamekeeper. Lawrence brilliantly conveys the ambivalent nature of the experience. Here is a description of the power of the orgasm:

> But it came with a strange slow thrust of peace, the dark thrust of peace and a ponderous primordial tenderness such as made the world in the beginning. . . heavier the billows of her rolled away to some shore, uncovering her, and closer and closer plunged the palpable unknown and further and further rolled the waves of herself away from herself, leaving her, till suddenly, in a quick shuddering convulsion, the quick of all her plasm was touched, she knew herself touched, the consummation was upon her, and she was gone. . . Ah too lovely, too lovely! In the ebbing she realized all the loveliness. (Lawrence, 1928)

The words have an almost religious feel to them but there is a bittersweet quality, too—"too lovely." This tone is accentuated earlier in the same twelfth chapter:

> It was quite true, as some poets said, that the God who created man must have had a sinister sense of humor, creating him a reasonable being, yet forcing him to take this ridiculous posture, and driving him with blind craving for this ridiculous performance (Lawrence, 1928).

Lawrence reveals brilliantly the Janus head of sexuality. There is a paradox between the ethereal qualities of sex and its potential to provoke utter degradation if mishandled. I think our two artists would have agreed. Doris Lessing, the Nobel Laureate novelist and feminist author of *The Golden Notebook*, related what a relief it was in later life, as the flame of passion guttered, to be   rid of the tyranny of sex on one's actions. Yet no-one can deny the unique wonder of the bond of a physical union between a man and woman committed together by true love and with the prospect of creating new life. It is perhaps life's greatest gift?

CONCLUSIONS

One has recounted the bare facts of the lives and interrelationship of probably the two greatest painters of the Post Impressionist Era. Both of them were ridden by the muse of painting to untimely deaths. They were two very different personalities united by a similar passion to express their visual senses. Vincent was introspective and religious in his view of the world while Paul was extrovert and pagan. They both ended up destitute, alone, conscious of their own apparent total failure and died premature deaths. The world has benefited hugely by the images left behind by them in their individual crusades.

Answer: We may agree with Schopenhauer that Art, working through the Senses, can allow us to escape the tyrannies of the Will to find meaning and the same may be true of loving sex— however one must be aware of the risks of the "left-hand path."

Reading List and Sources

Gauguin. The Quest for Paradise. Francoise Cachin. Harry N. Abrams Inc. New York. English translation 1992

Van Gogh. The Passionate Eye. Pascal Bonafoux. Publishers; Thames and Hudson. English translation 1992

Chapter 5. The Mystics

Carl Jung and Mircea Eliade

Question: Mysticism is claimed to give a direct link to a
transcendent sphere of life with esoteric meaning, but is this mere
poetry whose meaning is too uncertain to be of positive value?

Carl Jung

Mysticism, as a term, has been used to refer to those forms of experience
in which transcendent information, that is transformed into outer visions
and auditions or an inner unitive experience, reaches the mystic's psyche
directly rather than being mediated through the world. This description
certainly applies to Carl Jung whose inner life was as important as or even
more important to him than his outer life. For example, he felt that he was
in fact two persons. One was his outer persona of the parson's son and doctor with all his weaknesses, insecurities and ambitions. The second inner
person was an old man from another century, whom he describes as "skepti-
cal, mistrustful, and remote from the world of men but close to nature, the
earth, the sun, the moon." (Jung, 1962)

It was the second personality that received dreams and visions; they
gave Jung a sense of peace and inner security.

Jung's Life

Jung was born in 1875 in a small village on Lake Constance in Switzerland. His father was a minister in the Swiss Reformed Church, a position

which he had needed to take for financial reasons after an earlier academic career in which he had achieved a PhD in Philology and Linguistics. He was apparently prone to depression and this seemed to be associated with his inner questioning of his own religious faith. Jung appeared to inherit his mystical sense from his mother who had a mysterious aspect to her personality—indeed Jung suspected she had a dual personality herself. It was not a happy marriage unfortunately. It was rumored that Jung's paternal grandfather was the illegitimate son of Goethe, the German poet and dramatist-Jung apparently did nothing to dispel this suggestion.

After much deliberation, Jung studied medicine at the University of Basel qualifying in 1900. He came to realize that the specialty of Psychiatry would allow him to combine his interests in science and spirituality. On qualifying he took up a post as assistant physician at the Burghölzli, the Psychiatric hospital of the University of Zurich, under the eminent neurologist Eugene Bleuler. In 1905 he achieved the position of lecturer in psychiatry and senior physician. He put down this post in 1909 to give himself to his budding private practice and to his writing career. In 1902 he had married Emma who herself trained as an analyst. She had private means, which allowed Jung greater freedom in his eventual career.

Jung's Medical Career in Psychiatry

Bleuler encouraged Jung's interest in Schizophrenia: the "split mind," then known as Dementia Praecox and in 1906 he completed a monograph on "The Psychology of Dementia Praecox." In that work he acknowledged his indebtedness to the writings of Sigmund Freud and particularly Freud's book *The Interpretation of Dreams*. The two men developed a strong professional relationship from 1906 in the form of frequent letters and occasional meetings. Freud appeared to view Jung as the heir to his work on psychoanalysis of the unconscious mind. Freud's sphere of influence was mainly in the Jewish world—he anticipated that Carl would allow it to percolate into the gentile sphere. This historical interrelationship ended in disillusionment for both of them around 1913 leading to both men developing depressive manifestations. In Jung's case this lasted for approximately five years during which he felt a blockage to his abilities to write, lecture, make public appearances, and even to engage in reading. It was however a time that he felt developed his inner life, albeit, in a way which threatened to destroy him.

Jung's Contributions to Psychiatry

Jung developed his own system of analysis which he termed analytical psychology, as opposed to Freud's method of psychoanalysis. He placed much more emphasis on the individual response rather than a set response. He developed word association tests to elicit personal reactions which gave a clue to neurosis or psychosis. Like Freud he emphasized the importance of the interpretation of dreams, but considered the dream images tended to be special to the subject's own life history rather than a general interpretation. He talked of the "subconscious" mind rather than Freud's "unconscious" mind. Freud's unconscious mind harbored repressions which could surface to cause mental illness. In Jung's view, one's personal subconscious tends to harbor complexes: emotionally-charged ideas which have gone below the surface of the mind. However, they were not necessarily destructive and could act creatively if seen in the right light by the subject. They could be identified by word association tests and used creatively in the subjects' therapy. Jung started to become identified as the guru of his era so that privileged patients from all over the western world found their way to his consulting room to see the great man.

Jung's Environment

During a lecturing commitment in Zurich, my host took me to Kusnacht on the Lower Lake, a small, charming town where Jung lived and carried out his practice. The Jung home is not identified in any way for the general public because it is still inhabited by the Jung family. I stood at the foot of the long garden pathway between yew trees leading to the front door and tried to visualize the eminent persons who had trod that path to seek help with their inner problems, or complexes as Jung would term them. Later we journeyed to the little village of Bollingen on the Upper Lake, remote from the city. It was here that Jung built, often with his own hands, "the tower," a primitive habitation without heating or running water. There Jung would spend long periods of introspection. As an aid to thought, he loved to sail his small boat on the lake where there are wonderful views of the snow-covered Alps. He would carve images from his visionary life on stone so that the whole area came to have a sacred atmosphere to him. Frequently he was accompanied by his mistress, Toni Wolff—this was a relationship reluctantly sanctioned by his wife Emma, who seemed to realize that there was a side to his life for which she herself could not adequately cater. Jung acknowledged Toni's important role in his later creative writings and work. The Tower, and its late extensions, are not accessible to the public and again are inhabited by members of the Jung family. It was however deserted on our visit and my wife Carmen and I were able to wander throughout the grounds unauthorized, sensing the atmosphere of the place (its "genius loci" as the Romans used to call it). It was particularly evocative to stand on the small beach where Jung would have brought in his sailing boat at the end of the day.

Extrovertism/ Introvertism

In psychology, Jung described several entities which have come to be associated with him, particularly Extrovertism/Introvertism, the concept of the Collective Unconscious Mind, the Archetypes, the Symbols of Man, and the Process of Individuation.

The terms Extrovert and Introvert were first coined by Jung as part of a detailed classification of personality. They have come to be used widely in everyday life. Jung felt that both terms could be applicable to a well rounded personality, although implying a certain duality as in his own case. One needed to develop a certain degree of extrovertism in order to succeed in the outer world, but one's inner life was all important, requiring a degree of introvertism.

The Collective Unconscious Mind

In addition to the personal subconscious mind there was also the collective unconscious which was inherited or acquired as a trace of man's whole hominid history. The collective mind is peopled with potent images termed archetypes which can surface in dreams and images. They can be a potent source of creative and poetic activity. The concept of the inheritance of acquired mental concepts is, of course, highly controversial in modern genetics which denies the possibility of the inheritance of physical characteristics as claimed in the early 19th century by Jean Baptiste Lamarck, the eminent French naturalist. The musical sphere, however gives many examples of the apparent inheritance of potent musical ability in child prodigies. Jung compared his archetypes to Plato's "ideas," Schopenhauer's "ideas" and Kant's "categories." Kant himself believed in a priori contents of the mind as opposed to Locke's concept of the "tabula rasa" (the newborn mind is devoid of prior content). This relates to the essential divide in philosophy between rationalism and empiricism.

The Archetypes

Jung wrote: "The concept of the archetype, which is an indispensable correlate of the idea of the collective unconscious, indicates the existence of definite forms in the psyche which seem to be present always and everywhere" (Jung, 1962).

The Archetype is defined as an "imprint." Particularly characteristic archetypes can be listed as follows:

The Persona: this is the mask that we or others may present to the outside world like the literal mask worn in classical Greek drama.

The Shadow: this is the darkest side of our personality. We can easily project it unconsciously onto other people.

The Anima and the Animus: a man has in his subconscious an image termed the Anima who is the essence of the female within him. When he meets a woman who corresponds with his Anima figure, they may fall hopelessly in love at first sight. The comparable archetype in the female is the Animus, the woman's image of man.

The Mother Archetype: this archetype may have religious connotations such as The Great Mother, The Mother of God, The Virgin, and Sophia in western religion. In the East, as in Hinduism, the image may variously be Parvati (all female sweetness), Durga (all energy), or Kali (all ferocity with bloodstained fangs).

The Child: this may take the form of a child god or a child hero like the young Christ in the Temple or Krishna, the wonder performing avatar in Hinduism.

The Wise Old Man: may present in such forms as a magician, a king, a priest, a professor, or a sage. Jung would often encounter such an image in his own dreams of an ancient bearded sage whom he called Philemon being a source of wisdom and inspiration to him.

The Self: this Jung described as "the midpoint of the personality." The self, Jung confided is the "God within us".

The Symbols of Man

A symbol is a term, a name, or even a picture which possesses specific connotations in addition to its conventional and obvious meaning. Jung explained: "It has a wider "unconscious" aspect that is never precisely defined or fully explained. As the mind explores the symbol it is led to ideas that lie beyond the grasp of reason" (Jung 1962).

One of Jung's books was entitled *Symbols of Transformation*, where he identified the roles of symbols in his patients' inner lives. Jung had always avoided writing a text for the general reader, but towards the end of his life had a vision which instructed him that he must do so. This bestselling book was entitled *Man and His Symbols*, presenting the concept that man is a symbol making creature. The Process of Individuation is a process by which an individual may achieve full intellectual and spiritual development. It implies "coming to selfhood" or "self-realization." It does not come to everyone. Jung stated that "only those individuals who can attain to a higher degree of consciousness, are destined to it and called to it from the beginning, i.e., who have a capacity and an urge for higher differentiation." He maintained that sadly the great majority of human beings are still in the state of childhood and are notoriously unconscious.

Jung and Religion

Religion preoccupied Jung although his attitude to it was the reverse of conventional. A seminal quotation is,

"Everything to do with religion, everything it is and asserts, touches the human soul so closely that psychology least of all can afford to overlook it." (Jung 1962)

Jung believed that the loss of belief in an increasingly secular age left a great vacuum in the human psyche. He turned his mind to the spectrum of religion and one of his collected works in entitled *Psychology of Religion West and East*. He recognized the role of symbols and archetypes in religious mythology and practice. When asked whether he believed in God, he is reported to have replied, "I believe that there is a God Archetype in the human psyche." (Jung, 1962) As previously stated, the term "archetype" is seen as an imprint, and obviously an imprint requires an imprinting agency.

Comment

Jung opens to us a world of the mystical i.e. a search and contact with the numinous. I recently asked a colleague who is a psychologist whether Jung is now taken seriously as a scientist. He replied, "I think he is more of a poet." The work of both Freud and Jung is now to be seen to lack in scientific proof. Both have been major figures in psychological debate. Jung can be seen to be the mystic and Freud the pragmatist. But Jung is enormously helpful in trying to understand the vast spectrum of world religions. His concept of universal archetypes helps one to appreciate equivalence in different religions. Think of the seaport cities of Asia, where one might see statues of the Virgin Mary as part of the Catholic tradition brought by Portuguese explorers just streets away from representations of Kuan-Yin, the Buddhist bodhisattva of compassion, in the half open doors of homes in the older Chinese sections of the town. It is easy to see that these were two equivalent images of female love and compassion equating with the Mother archetype. A product of the Jungian tradition is the recent text by two Jungian therapists, Anne Baring and Jules Cashford, entitled *The Myth of the Goddess—Evolution of an Image.* (Baring and Cashford, 1991).

MIRCEA ELIADE

Mircea Eliade was a contemporary of Jung, although thirty-five years younger. Eliade was Romanian, having been born in Bucharest in 1907 as the son of an army officer. He was a major historian of religion, a philosopher, a fiction writer and an academic professor. His brilliance developed very early so that at the age of 18 years, he celebrated the appearance of his 100th published article. He was stated to be fluent in five languages (Romanian, French, German, Italian, and English) and had a good working knowledge of three others (Hebrew, Persian, and Sanskrit). When the two men first met at a conference in Switzerland in 1950 they realized that they had a great bond of common feeling, although both of them were familiar with each other's writings before this.

Eliade's life prior to this had been full of event. He obtained a degree in philosophy at the University of Bucharest. He set out on a career as a journalist and essayist. He was obviously a passionate young man, and his vigorous intellect involved him in some activities which were later seen to be less then discrete. He began teaching in Bucharest as an assistant to the philosopher Nae Ionesco, who was also a leading figure in a Romanian right wing nationalist organization known as the Legionary Movement. This movement initially had fascist leanings which endangered Eliade's reputation, rather as in the case of the German philosopher Heidegger. Eliade was arrested in 1938 after a crack down on the so called Iron Guard authorized by King Carol II, resulting in his being kept for three weeks in a cell. He regained favor with the administration and indeed was made cultural attaché to the United Kingdom, and he later took a similar post in Portugal. As the communist regime took hold in Romania, Eliade went into exile in France. Some of his important early writings were undertaken often working in the hum-drum setting of a kitchen table—it is said that he would often work for as long as fifteen hours a day.

Interlude in India

As an interlude in 1928, Eliade obtained a four year scholarship to go to study in India at the University of Calcutta. His tutor was Professor Surendranath Dasgupta, an eminent professor at the university and past Cambridge graduate being the author of a five volume "History of Indian Philosophy." Indian religion made a great impression of Eliade, which was to influence him for the rest of his career. Eliade's passionate and perhaps indiscrete nature came to the fore again; he fell in love with his tutor's daughter and had a passionate physical relationship with her which he later recorded in an autobiographical novel untitled *Bengal Nights*. This led to his having to leave India prematurely—although it taught him about sensuality as one side of his nature.

Cosmic Religious Feeling

Eliade was deeply impressed by the religious nature of the whole of life in India as he saw it expressed by simple peasant people in the environment of their villages. I myself, in my four visits to India, was similarly impressed by how ordinary objects and events were seen in a sacred context. Eliade saw that this was particularly so in relationship to the mystery of growing plants and animals within the context of agriculture. Country folk viewed the world, as he put it, as "an unbroken cycle of life, death, and rebirth" (Eliade, 1957).

Eliade came to call this "archaic religion" and also used the term "cosmic religious feeling." He later came to realize that this sort of viewpoint stretched from the villages of India to those of his own Romania, from Europe and Scandinavia to East Asia, the Americas and other locales where primitive people tilled the soil as ancestors had taught them for generations. Nature itself was sacred—he called this the sacrality of nature. He later came to appreciate that the Christian peasants of his own native Romania and other central European lands had a similar attitude which he entitled "Cosmic Christianity," whereby Jesus was seen not so much as a historical figure but as equating with the resurrecting deities of the ancient world who would die, spend a period in the underworld and then show rebirth in the same way that the plant world dies down in the winter, is preserved in the moist earth as seed or root and then breaks forth again in the spring time. It is difficult from Eliade's writings to detect clearly his own inner most religious convictions but all the indications are that his sympathies lay with this type of "cosmic religious feeling" rather than the more formal features of his background of the Russian Orthodox Church.

Eliade's Major Works

Two major monographs particularly impressed Jung and are mentioned in many of his own works. These were:

• *Yoga: Immortality and Freedom.*

This provides a detailed discussion of those yogic techniques that he had experienced in various ashrams in India particularly meditation, concentration, asanas, pranayama and yoga in relationship to Brahmanism, Buddhism, Tantrism, Oriental alchemy and Shamanism. This was first published in French in 1933.

• *Shamanism: Archaic Techniques of Ecstasy.*

The shaman is the earliest religious figure who is at once magician and medicine man, healer and miracle worker, priest, mystic and poet. The shaman is his initiation undergoes very frequently a symbolic death plus resurrection and claims the ability later to leave his body and to visit the realms of all life and death. This work records this religious phenomenon at its origin in Siberia and Central Asia, tracing its occurrence elsewhere in Asia, the Pacific Islands, the Americas and among the ancient Indo-European people.

Eliade's greatest achievement is the monumental three-volume *A History of Religious Ideas.* The scope of this work can be seen from the three titles, namely:

Volume One: From the Stone Age to the Eleusinian Mysteries.

Volume Two: From Gautama Buddha to the Triumph of Christianity.

Volume Three: From Muhammad to the Age of Reforms.

Eliade records the main movements in the whole of man's religious history from its archaic roots to modern times. The intensity of this enterprise had a marked physical toll for him unfortunately as he records in the Preface of the third volume: "The delay with which this third volume appears is due to reasons of health: as time goes by my vision continues to dwindle and because of a stubborn arthritis I write with difficulty. This obliges me to complete this last part with the collaboration of several of my colleagues, selected from among my former students" (Eliade, 1985).

This is indeed the hallmark of that breed of pioneer whose dedication drives him to complete his life's task whatever the cost to himself. Eliade was greatly supported throughout his whole life and particularly towards the end by his wife Christinel, to whom he dedicates each of these historic volumes.

Eliade and the University of Chicago

In 1957 Eliade was invited to give a series of lectures at the University of Chicago organized by the scholar Joachim Wach. After these lectures, and on Wach's untimely death, Eliade was appointed as his replacement as Distinguished Service Professor of the History of Religions. He and Wach were recognized as the founders of the so-called "Chicago School" of religious education that basically was said to have defined the study of religions for the second half of the twentieth century. Eliade has said that when he came to Chicago, there were three significant professorships in the history of religions in the United States; twenty years later, there were thirty, half of which were occupied by his own students! One of Eliade's further great achievements while in Chicago was to act as editor-in-chief of the monumental *Encyclopedia of Religion* which comprised seventeen volumes covering every aspect of religion by leading scholars in the field constituting the standard reference encyclopedia on religion. This was published in 1987, the year following his death.

The Meetings of Jung and Eliade at the Eranos Conferences in Switzerland

Eliade met Jung in 1950 at the Eranos Conference and came to realize their strong fellow feelings and links. In a contemporary photograph the younger Eliade gazes in an attitude almost of veneration at the white-haired figure of Jung who seems to personify his own archetypal figure of the Wise Old Man. The Eranos Conferences were organized by Olga Frobe-Kapteyn, a somewhat eccentric but fortunately very rich widow, whose father had left her a large house, the Casa Gabriele, with extensive grounds in a village outside Ascona on the shores of Lake Maggiore. In this idyllic setting she built a Conference Center which was planned to be a spiritual center designed to be "undenominational, nonsectarian and open to esoteric thinkers and occult students of all groups in Europe and elsewhere." Eliade describes his emotions in interrelating with Jung: "I felt I was listening to a Chinese sage or an East European peasant, still rooted in Earth Mother yet close to Heaven at the same time." (Eliade, 1988)

This led to a series of visits; often Eliade would visit Jung at the family home at Kusnacht—I well remember standing outside that august home during my own visit to Switzerland and contemplating their meetings there.

The Links Between Jung and Eliade

Jung doubtless found comfort and fulfillment in his relationship with Eliade. His whole life had been disrupted after his parting of the ways with Freud, but now there was fellow feeling and agreement. Eliade, for all his major attainments, seemed to see himself as an acolyte to Jung, who stood as a Guru-like figure to him. The common points of their viewpoints can be summarized as involving particularly:

- The Importance of Archaic Religion.
- The Importance of Symbol and Myth.
- The Archetypes.

Both men were clearly mystics finding inspiration and empathy from the whole spectrum of man's religious heritage.

Answer: It appears that we may well have a mystical center(s) in our brain, as discussed in the section on Neuroscience, so that its exercise is clearly important for a full sense of meaning in our lives.

Reading List and Sources
On Jung. Anthony Stevens. Penguin Books. 1991.
Yoga. Mircea Eliade. Arkana. 1990.

CHAPTER 6. AGNOSTICS IN THE CAUSE OF EVOLUTION

Charles Darwin and Michael Behe

Question: Is agnosticism (or not being committed)
in the face of the facts of the evolutionary process, and
their likely meaning, moral cowardice, or is it only
reasonable in view of the current state of knowledge?

CHARLES DARWIN

To know where he stands in the world, a man needs to consider where he has come from. We may recall Gauguin's great painting "Where have we come from, What are we doing here, Where are we going." The published work of Charles Darwin scandalized the Victorian world of his time in that it stated that man (seen by the Christian world as made in the image of God) had descended from the realm of the apes. In a famous debate on evolution at the Oxford meeting of the British Association in 1860 the principle debater for the Church position Bishop Wilberforce (nicknamed "Soapy Sam") asked the celebrated question of Darwin's supporters: "Is it through his grandfather or his grandmother that he claims descent from a monkey?" (Huxley and Kettlewell, 1974)

T. H. Huxley, the eminent biologist speaking for Darwin, is said to have muttered, "The Lord hath delivered him into my hands." He stated that if he had to choose between a poor ape for an ancestor and a man of great influence, who used those gifts to introduce ridicule into a scientific discussion and to discredit humbled seekers of the truth, he would affirm his preference for the ape. The effect of all this on the audience was so great that one lady is said to have fainted in the general commotion. There is no doubt that the work of Darwin produced a sea change in the way in which we, as a species, view ourselves. It brought into the searchlight the whole question of man's evolution by a steady and prolonged process from the world of the animals, as opposed to the biblical concept of dramatic creation at the hands of God. Not only did it shake the composure of the whole world, it also shook Darwin's own convictions to make him an agnostic "but never an Atheist."

Initial Failure in the Two Noble Professions of Medicine and the Church

Darwin was born in 1809 into a well to do land owning family in Shrewsbury situated on the attractive river Severn in the border country of Wales. His father, Robert Waring Darwin, was a successful medical practitioner. His father's physical appearance was remarkable in that he was over six feet tall and weighed 24 stones (a stone is 14 pounds). His personality was similarly outstanding; he was "the kindest man I ever knew" (using Charles' own words), albeit that he was a confirmed Atheist. He had seen much suffering particularly in the poor areas of Shrewsbury; Charles reports him as saying "every road out of Shrewsbury is associated in my mind with some painful event"—indeed, he hated medicine in the way in which it was practiced in Victorian England.

Darwin was a mediocre student. He entered the University of Edinburgh (I know it well having been a professor there for eight years) to study medicine. After two years, Charles realized that he did not wish to become a physician and his father allowed him to return home. One must be aware of the crude nature of medicine in the early 19th century. As Darwin said himself, "I saw two very bad operations...but I ran away before they were completed" (Darwin 1887). The same spectacle of surgery without anesthesia had appalled the young poet John Keats around the same period, making him also quit medicine.

His father decided that he must enter another noble profession and qualify to become a minister in the Church. He spent three years at the University of Cambridge and managed to obtain a good pass degree. He realized, however, that he did not have the motivation to enter the Church, and regarded himself as a failure.

He was befriended by two professors, J.S. Henslow, a professor of botany, and Adam Sedgwick, professor of geology. They kindled in him a great interest in biology and related subjects so that he suddenly developed a sense of mission. In short, he was a late developer who needed the catalytic influence of others to light the blue touch paper of his enthusiasm. Such people may well be completely thrown aside by the present educational system which requires consistent high level grade point averages for a student to gain entry to higher education!

The Voyage of the Beagle

It was remarkable that Charles should be able to relate as an undergraduate student to such senior members of staff and it must be a testimony to the quality of his personality. It was through Professor Henslow that Darwin was invited to be a naturalist to the ship's company of the sailing vessel the Beagle. This was an epic journey taking the best part of five years (1831–1836). It circumnavigated the world allowing Charles to investigate the fauna, flora, and geological formations of many areas including South America, Australia, and the Pacific Islands. One high point in this itinerary was the Galapagos Islands off the coast of Ecuador. This presented a sequestered colony of animals and birds on small islands enabling him to trace the pattern of change from species on the South American mainland. Darwin was meticulous in keeping notebooks and collecting specimens so that his findings and chain of thought were carefully recorded. It was however 23 years before in 1859 he published his major work *On the Origin of Species by Means of Natural Selection* in which he formulated his conclusions. Why did it take him so long? If he were a university academic in the present era, his job would be on the line for lack of publications—fortunately, like Carl Jung, he had private means, which meant that he did not have to take a remunerated occupation. The reasons for the delay appeared to be that he needed time to gather full evidence for his revolutionary hypothesis; however, he also realized in 1858 that his fellow biologist Alfred Wallace was starting to produce a manuscript putting forward a similar theory.

Darwin's Revolutionary Ideas

What were Darwin's groundbreaking theories expounded in *The Origin* and his later book *The Descent of Man* (1871). It has become apparent that they come down to two major conclusions.

The Tree of Life; all organisms now alive on earth trace their origin back to a common ancestor. This pattern of descent includes man.

Natural Selection; the main cause for the similarities and differences that exist in the earth's biota (it's plant and animal species) lies in the process of Natural Selection.

Natural Selection can be seen to have three main components:

Variations will appear within a species often with no relationship initially to an adaptive advantage. Thus in a species of fox some animals will be lighter in their fur than others.

Some variations provide their bearers with an advantage in the struggle to live and reproduce within their environment. This was termed, by Herbert Spencer, a contemporary philosopher whose evolutionary ideas somewhat predated those of Darwin, "survival of the fittest." Thus in an arctic environment a fox with fur which approaches white in color will be better camouflaged than his fellow fox that has dark fur.

Variations are often transmitted to progeny through inheritance.

This process of Natural Selection came into Darwin's mind after reading *Essay on the Principle of Population* by Thomas Malthus (Published anonymously in 1798 and revised in 1803). This pointed out that populations tend to increase faster than the means of subsistence; this applies to animals and humans alike. Disastrous overpopulation and starvation has not, as yet, taken place humanly due to war, famine, disease, and infanticide i.e. the survival of those fittest to withstand these hazards.

Darwin had no knowledge of the underlying mechanisms of genetics in that genes had not been identified, nor was there, of course, any knowledge of the biochemistry of DNA. In his collected papers he had an essay by Gregor Mendel, an Austrian monk and biologist whose experiments on the breeding and hybridization of plants (particularly peas) were carried out in the garden of his monastery. The results were only published in a local journal (1866 and 1896) so that they did not become general knowledge until about 1900. They examined the characteristics of heredity in individual plants and Mendel discovered the statistical laws governing the transmission from parent to offspring of unit hereditary factors, which are now known to be the genes. However Darwin did not appear to have read the paper and certainly did not comment on it.

Why Did Darwin's Views Cause Such a Stir?

The official view of the Anglican Church of the time was that species could not change (they were immutable) for each species had been individually created by God himself, as detailed in Genesis, and man was a "special creation" who had been given dominion over the animal world. It must be admitted that not all Victorian intellectuals took the Genesis Creation narratives literally but less sophisticated religious people would regard Darwin as threatening the sacred text. In particular there were several disturbing questions:

What did it mean for man to be made in the image of God if we shared ancestors with other primates and indeed ultimately the whole animal world?

Had the human soul been added during the evolutionary process or was it more meaningful to speak of our being souls rather than having them?

What were the implications for moral values if the evolution of the moral sense could be explained purely in terms of survival value, without reference to the transcendent?

It took the Church some considerable time to come to terms with the theory of evolution. Pope Pius XII in his document Humani Generis (1950) stated:

> The Teaching Authority of the Church does not forbid that in conformity with the present state of human sciences and sacred theology, research and discussions, on the part of men experienced in both fields, take place with regard to the doctrine of evolution, in as far as it inquires into the origin of the human body as coming from preexistent and living matter—for the Catholic faith obliges us to hold that souls are immediately created by God. (Pope Pius XII, 1950)

In other words, evolution can be considered as a theory, but there was an act of creation when God inserted the soul into man. There was no suggestion as to when this may have taken place in the eyes of the Church authorities; one is mindful that Homo sapiens appear to have arisen as far back as 130,000 years ago in Africa. Was that when this all took place? Pope John Paul II in 1996 went further down the path of confirming the truth of evolution by stating:

It has been proven true; we always celebrate nature's factuality, and we look forward to interesting discussions of theological implication. (Pope John Paul II, 1997)

What Did All of This Do to Darwin Himself?

Darwin had started out on the Voyage of the Beagle as a conventional believer with an extensive knowledge of the bible. As he contemplated the apparently savage battle going on in the realm of nature for survival his view gradually changed. At first he was still a theist but with far from orthodox views. Later he became a confirmed Agnostic. His change of stance was accelerated by the tragic death of his daughter in childbirth at the age of 26. Here are reported replies to the repeated questions from the public about his religious views:

"I am sorry to have to inform you that I do not believe in the Bible as a divine revelation, and therefore not in Jesus Christ as the Son of God. I do not believe that there ever has been any Revelation. As for a future life, every man must judge for himself between conflicting, vague possibilities." (Darwin: Letter)

All of this produced a great deal of soul searching on the part of Charles, particularly as his beloved wife, Emma, was a conventional believer. He tried not to publicize his real beliefs for this reason particularly. He died at the age of 73, supported by Emma as always, of heart failure probably due to chronic Chevas' disease, a disease transmitted by the Great Black Bug of the Pampas (Benchuca), with which he is known to have come in contact during his time in South America. This disease could have well also accounted for his serious debility over many years, preventing him from working more often than one day in three. However, he was able to be very prolific in his researches and published work based in his beloved home of Down House in Kent. His works on corals, orchids, and the role of earthworms are classics. Down House is graced with a particularly evocative 'Thinking Path' where Darwin formulated most of his ground breaking ideas.

Final Assessment

Darwin had expected to be buried under the great yew tree in the churchyard in Down. He was however buried with full honors in Westminster Abbey, in the same environment as the man who has been stated to be his fellow greatest English scientist, namely Sir Isaac Newton. Darwin's views have changed virtually every aspect of science throughout the world with regard particularly to the role of natural selection in the evolution of almost every variety of activity. His concept of the tree of life means that we contemplate a union with all nature. This was new to the Western world although in the East, particularly in the Buddhist tradition there has always been a consciousness of the links between all sentient beings included in Samsara (the wheel of life).

The theory of evolution is now coming under new appraisal particularly in the view of the school of thought of Intelligent Design which is to be discussed later. Darwin's theories seemed to explain adequately the mechanisms of micro-evolution whereby variations in a species may help it to adapt to the environment. However it is still not proven how one species can change into another by the process of macro-evolution. None of this nullifies Darwin's enormous and courageous contribution to scientific and indeed religious thought. Like most great pioneers he suffered both mentally and physically in the path that he trod.

MICHAEL BEHE: THE SEARCH FOR THE LIMITS OF DARWINISM

It may seem ironic to include Michael Behe in a chapter on Darwin for he has been an active critic of Darwinism. He has been one of the most vocal spokesmen for the rival school of Intelligent Design which claims that life could not have arisen in all its complexity by random processes as Darwin suggested, but requires an underlying influence of Intelligence. In his 2007 book entitled *The Edge of Evolution: The Search for the Limits of Darwinism*, he sets out to exert some measure of compromise between Darwinism and Intelligent Design.

The basic steps in the progression of the School of Intelligent Design can be traced as follows:

Sir Fred Hoyle questioned the underlying mathematics of Darwinism in his book "The Intelligent Universe" in 1983. We discuss Hoyle's seminal viewpoint in detail in Chapter 12.

The biochemist and medical doctor Michael Denton criticized the archeological evidence for Darwinism in his book *Evolution: A Theory in Crisis* in 1986.

Michael Behe, the biochemist, published his book *Darwin's Black Box: The Biochemical Challenge to Evolution* in 1986, wherein he claimed that many biochemical processes were too complex (irreducibly complex) to be explained by random processes.

William Dembski, a theologian and a mathematician, followed up Hoyle's criticism of the mathematical basis of Darwinism in his book *The Design Inference* in 1998.

Philip Johnson, an analytic lawyer, examined the evidence for Darwinism as one might in a court of law in his book *Evolution as Dogma* in 1990. His verdict found against Darwin and his theory.

Michael Denton in his book *Evolution: A Theory in Crisis* sums up his basic doubts in the preface on the cover of the book as follows:

> Although the theory appears to be correct regarding the emergence of a new species, its larger claims to account for the relationship between classes and orders, let alone the origin of life, appeared to be based on shaky foundations at best. Not only has paleontology failed to come up with the fossil "missing links" which Darwin anticipated, but hypothetical reconstructions of major evolutionary developments—such as those linking birds to reptiles—are beginning to look more like fantasies than serious conjectures. Even the currently popular theory of "Punctuated Equilibrium" cannot adequately fill in the real gaps we face when envisioning how major groups of plants and animals arose. Most important of all, the discoveries of molecular biologists, far from strengthening Darwin's claims are throwing more and more doubt on traditional Darwinism. (Denton 1993)

Who is Michael Behe?

Behe is professor of biochemistry at Lehigh University in Pennsylvania. He worked at the National Institute of Health from 1978–1982 carrying out work on the structure of DNA. Subsequently, he was assistant professor of chemistry at Queens College in New York City. His advocacy of Intelligent Design has thrown his career into considerable hazard. Even the Department of Biological Sciences at his own university has published an official disclaimer of his work, stating: "It is our collective position that intelligent design has no basis in science, has not been tested experimentally, and should not be regarded as scientific." (Lehigh University 1998)

One must be mindful that the whole of the scientific community in the Western world is wedded to the concept of Darwinism which permeates every field of science and even sociology and political theory. If someone throws a spanner in the works, it is likely to provoke a violent reaction, as so many pioneers have found to their detriment. While the scientific community in general is up in arms against him, he has a considerable following in the general public, to whom he aimed his two main books; his latest book is a bestseller. Behe acknowledges that he is a Catholic and believes in God as the Intelligence behind life, although he is prepared to look at other explanations. Indeed, he is most recently recognizing some of the limitations of his viewpoint, verging on an agnostic stance, as we shall see.

Behe's Book: Darwin's Black Box

The main thrust of this book is that many biological mechanisms are irreducibly complex at a molecular level and cannot be explained by natural selection against a background of random mutations. Behe explains what he means by this term as follows: "By irreducibly complex I mean a single system composed of several well-matched, interacting parts that contribute to the basic function, wherein the removal of any one of the parts causes the system to effectively cease functioning." (Behe 1996)

He tells us that an irreducibly complex system cannot be produced directly (that is, by continuously improving the initial function, which continues to work by the same mechanism) by slight successive modifications of a precursor system, because any precursor to an irreducibly complex system that is missing a part is by definition nonfunctional. Therefore, an irreducibly complex biological system, if there is such a thing, would be a powerful challenge to Darwinian evolution. As an object of common experience, Behe sites a mouse trap as an object which is irreducibly complex in that it cannot function unless all its parts are intact. The individual parts cannot function alone.

He emphasizes that from a biological viewpoint there are a multitude of structures and biochemical processes which appear to be irreducibly complex but discusses three in particular:

• The Cilium: Many cells have cilia and these are amazingly complex. For example sperm use cilia to allow them to swim.

• The Bacterial Flagellum: This is like a small rotary motor which allows a bacterium to swim. It contains over two hundred different kinds of proteins to allow it to function.

• The Blood Clotting System: This is a very complex series of stages or cascades divided into an intrinsic pathway and an extrinsic pathway.

These claims have been like a red rag to a bull to conventional scientists. No less an authority than Francis Collins, erstwhile head of The Human Genome Project, has raised genetic objections to Behe's claims. He states that the similarity in the proteins in the clotting cascade can be shown to reflect ancient gene duplications that then allowed the new copy unfettered by a need to maintain its original function (since the old copy was still doing that) to gradually evolve to take on a new function, driven by the force of natural selection. With regard to the flagellum he states: "Comparison of protein sequences from multiple bacteria has demonstrated that several components of the flagellum are related to an entirely different apparatus used by certain bacteria to inject toxins into other bacteria that they are attacking" (Collins, 2006). Thus Behe has raised a huge rumpus which has threatened to sacrifice his whole career.

Behe's Book, The Edge of Evolution and the Search for the Limits of Darwinism

In his new book, Behe is much more conciliatory. I think that he is conscious of the great debate that has been aroused and the need to provide some sort of compromise. He agrees to the three elements that are part of Darwin's theory, namely:

- Common Descent from a Single Ancestor of All Life.
- The Process of Natural Selection.
- The Influence of Random Mutations.

He acknowledges that these processes take place but discusses in great detail how much or how little of the evolutionary process is occupied by them. Current studies are great reminders that random mutation and natural selection can account for many relatively minor changes in life—not only changes in invisible metabolic pathways like antibiotic resistance in rats or malaria, but also changes in the appearance of animals.

> The different sizes and shapes of dogs, the patterns of coloration of insect wings, and more can very likely be attributed to Darwinian processes affecting gene switches. We can conclude that animal design probably extends into life at least as far as vertebrate classes, maybe deeper, and that random mutations likely explain differences at least up to the species level, perhaps somewhat beyond. (Behe, 2007)

Behe comes to the conclusion that somewhere between the level of vertebrate species and class lies the organismal edge of Darwinian evolution.

The book provides a vertical scale with three sections:

- The Surprising Depth of Fine-tuning of Nature for Life on Earth: This is by far the largest part of the scale where he sees the influence of design in the following: laws of nature, physical constants, ratios of fundamental constants, amount of matter in the universe, speed of expansion in the universe, properties of elements such as carbon, properties of chemicals such as water, the location of the solar system in the galaxy, the location of planets in the solar system, origin and properties of earth/moon, properties of biochemicals such as DNA, origin of life, cells, genetic code, multiprotein complexes, molecular machines, biological kingdoms, developmental genetic programs, integrated protein networks, phyla, cell types, classes.

• The Tentative Edge of Random Evolution: Here he includes Orders, Families, Genera.

• Contingency in Biology: This is where he feels that natural selection and random mutations may be responsible in the following cases: Species, Varieties, Individuals, Environmental Accidents.

HOW WOULD DARWIN AND BEHE HAVE GOT ON TOGETHER?

Darwin was a very honest and self critical man all too aware of some of the implications of his theory. He would have been interested in Behe's examination of the multiple universe concept as expounded by the Oxford philosopher, Nick Bistro. The usual form of the hypothesis is that our universe is but one in a vast ensemble of actually existing universes, the totality of which we call the multiverse. The fine-tuning that Behe notes (the so called anthropic principle) might only be found in one amongst many universes. However, Behe rejects this hypothesis as unhelpful and wasteful—I think Darwin would have been relieved! Both men came from a Christian background although, as stated, Darwin felt that he must change his position to that of an agnostic. Both men were very aware of the possible implications of their findings for the image of any Creator behind the life. Behe quotes Darwin in a letter to Asa Gray with regard to the question of Ichneumon Flies which lay their eggs inside the body of butterfly caterpillars: "I cannot persuade myself that a beneficent and omnipotent god would have designedly created the Ichneumonidae with the express intention of their feeding within the living body of caterpillars" (Darwin: Letter to Asa Gray).

Behe is also a very honest man, like Darwin. He realizes that there is design evident even in the malign malaria parasite, which he has studied extensively. Behe muses, however: "Are viruses and parasites part of some brilliant, as-yet-unappreciated economy of nature, or do they reflect the bungling of an incompetent designer? Maybe the designer isn't all that beneficent or omnipotent. Science can't answer questions like that, but denying design simply because it can cause terrible pain is a failure of nerve, a failure to look the universe fully in the face." (Behe 2007)

That is honesty indeed and the kind of attitude that we must try to adopt in our frank search for meaning. It is apparent that contemplation of evolution turned Darwin into an agnostic and even beyond and is now tipping the balance for Behe.

> Answer: A frank consideration of Intelligent Design
> is essential to perceiving the meaning behind Nature. It
> is currently being identified with biblical Creationism,
> which is totally the reverse of the insight of its original
> proponent, Sir Fred Hoyle, as we shall describe later.

Reading List and Sources

The Cambridge Companion to Darwin. Edited by Jonathan Hodge and Gregory Ridick. Cambridge University Press. 2003.

The Edge of Evolution. The Search for the Limits of Darwinism. Michael Behe. Free Press 2007.

CHAPTER 7. THE PRIMATOLOGISTS

Frans De Wall and Barbara King
Question: If we accept descent from the Great Apes,
is there meaning in examining their behavior in order
to seek the roots of our own highest functions?

Primates are a taxonomic order amongst the animals to which apes and humans belong. The primatologist studies this order but particularly with regard to the Apes, in order to better understand the human condition. The primates are divided into two major groups namely the prosimians ("pre-monkeys") and the anthropoids ("like humans"). The primates are considered to have arisen around 65 million years ago from an ancestral mammalian stock.

The most important features of the primates are the following:
• grasping hands
• forward-facing eyes
• large brains
• lengthy period of learning

The Prosimians have few other features that resemble us. The most important examples are the nocturnal slow Loris found in India and Sri Lanka and the ring-tailed lemur from Madagascar, the major island off the East African coast. The Anthropoids appear to have diverged from the line of other primates about 30 to 40 million years ago. They comprise, in evolutionary order, the monkeys, the apes, and the hominids (man-like creatures). An anatomical difference between monkeys and apes is that monkeys have tails whereas apes do not. Apes resemble man much more closely than the monkeys particularly with regard to their number of chromosomes, the configuration of their muscles and skeletal elements and their behavioral complexity, particularly intelligence.

IS MAN AN ACCIDENT OF EVOLUTION OR ITS INTENDED GOAL?

The dinosaurs monopolized the earth for around 150 million years and might have continued to do so unless they were wiped out by some form of global catastrophe. The most common theory for the nature of that catastrophe was the collision of a major asteroid with the earth some 65 million years ago causing huge dust storms that blotted out the light from the sun. The prominent paleontologist Steven Jay Gould believed that if this event had not taken place it is likely man never would have evolved, saying: "We must assume that consciousness would not have evolved on our planet if a cosmic catastrophe had not claimed the dinosaurs as victims. In an entirely literal sense, we owe our existence, as large and reasoning mammals, to our lucky stars." (Gould, 1990)

During the era of the dinosaurs, there were a number of species of small and inconspicuous mammals also inhabiting the planet. With the demise of the dinosaurs these mammals were enabled to diversify eventually giving rise to the primates and eventually ourselves. It should increase our humility as a species to consider that we might merely be an accident!

WHO ARE OUR TWO PRIMATOLOGISTS?

Frans De Wall is a biologist and ethologist, recognized worldwide for his work on the social intelligence of such primates as chimpanzees, bonobos, capuchins, and macaques. He is Professor in the Psychology department of Emory University and Director of the Living Links Center at the Yerkaes Primates Center in Atlanta. His seminal book in 2005 is entitled "Our Inner Ape: an Explanation of Why We Are Who We Are." Our second Primatologist, Barbara King, is Professor of Anthropology at the College of William and Mary. She is a biological anthropologist, who has studied ape and monkey behavior in Gabon, Kenya, and the Smithsonian Institution's National Geographic Park. Her 2007 book is entitled *Evolving God: A Provocative View of the Origins of Religion*. She is the junior of our two authors and expresses her indebtedness to the work of Frans Dewall but provides a different perspective on the material under study.

THE TREE OF LIFE AND THE MISSING LINK

Both writers agree on the Tree of Origin of humans and the four great apes (orangutan, gorilla, bonobo, and chimpanzee). The orangutan diverged from this path of origin about 14 million years ago, and the gorilla about 7.5 million years ago. The human line diverged about 5.5 million years ago leaving the chimpanzees and the bonobos to form a single genus termed Pan. They diverged from each other around 2.5 million years ago. It is generally considered that among the apes, our closest kin are chimps and bonobos, neither one of which is closer to us than the other. It has been argued that since bonobos never left the humid jungle (whereas chimpanzees did so partially) and our own ancestors did so completely, bonobos probably have encountered fewer pressures to change from us. They may therefore look most like the forest ape from which we both descended—sometimes called the Missing Link.

OUR CLOSEST KIN ARE THE CHIMPS AND BONOBOS

It is estimated that there may be only 200 thousand chimpanzees left in the wild and about 20 thousand bonobos. Chimpanzees are the larger of the two animals weighing 66–130 pounds and being located mainly in West and Central Africa. The bonobo is smaller (its alternative name is pygmy chimpanzee) weighing up to 86 pounds with its main location being in Central Africa. If these two species are our nearest cousins, how do they differ in temperament? The fact is that they are very different indeed! The chimpanzee society is male dominated and disagreements are settled by aggression. They mainly eat fruit, leaves, flowers, and seeds but occasionally raiding parties will cooperate to kill and eat animal prey such as monkeys, birds, and even small antelopes. Social bonds may last for years but there are no long-term male-female bonds for reproduction. On the other hand in bonobo society, the female is dominant and disagreements tend to be settled by sexual activity! Bonobos feed chiefly on the ground mainly on fruits and seeds, but also on leaves, flowers, fungi, and eggs, and only occasionally small animals. The latter activity is quite uncommon and in general bonobos are more peaceful and nonviolent. Sexual relations are common between males, females, and young in various combinations and may be used to ease social tension. De Wall sums it all up: "The power-hungry and brutal chimp contrasts with the peace-loving and erotic bonobo—a kind of

Dr. Jekyll and Mr. Hyde. Our own nature is an uneasy marriage of the two." (De Wall 2005)

It certainly behooves us to remember the bonobo in our nature. The French referred to bonobos as Left Bank chimpanzees and primatologists jokingly used the phrase "We're gonna bonobo tonight"! The alternative of the chimp killer image is a forbidding one and DeWall points out that 160 million people in the 20th century lost their lives at the hands of their own species due to war, genocide, and political oppression. It seems, we are bi-polar in our inheritance and we ought to be aware of it.

THE CHAIN OF HOMINID ANCESTORS

The science of paleontology has revealed (on the basis of discovered fos-sils and radio-isotope dating) the following basic timeline of human precur-sor species leading to modern man:

1. The Australopithecines. *Australopithecus afarensis* lived between 3.9 and 3 million years ago. It was one of the first hominids to stand upright—it was bipedal. Its brain capacity was about 450 cc and it was between 3'6" and 5' in height. Mary Leakey discovered a set of footprints of this species embed-ded in solidified volcanic ash in the Olduvai Gorge in Laetoli in Tanzania. A male and female, almost certainly, walked side by side, perhaps holding hands and witnessing the volcano eruption itself. There is some suggestion of the footprints of a child or smaller individual skipping in and out of the footprints of the older couple. It is one of the most evocative findings in the whole of paleontology. What was the reaction of the early hominids to this natural disaster? How much were they capable of comprehending, and how much did it mean to them? Remember their brain capacity was about 450cc i.e., about a third of modern brain capacity.

2. *Homo habilis*. This species has been nicknamed the "handyman" be-cause stone tools have been found adjacent to its fossil remains. This species existed between 2.4 and 1.5 million years ago. Brain capacity rose in later discovered specimens to about 800 cc and height was about 5 feet.

3. *Homo erectus*. This species existed between 1.8 million and 300 thou-sand years ago, being very successful in that it persisted for approximately a million and a half years. Brain size could vary from approximately 900 cc up to approaching the same size as modern man at around 1,200 cc. Its behavior appears to have been more sophisticated including the use of characteristic hand axes. It seems certain that Erectus had discovered fire and cooking. He

was approximately the same size as modern man but sturdier in build, and likely to have been much stronger.

4. *Homo sapiens neanderthalensis.* This species existed mainly in Europe and the Middle East between 150,000 to 35,000 years ago. Its brain size exceeded that of modern man at about 1,450 cc. It not clear whether cross breeding with *Homo sapiens sapiens* occurred. The Neanderthals were around 5'6" in height with a very heavy, powerful bodily habitus. The Neanderthals coexisted with both archaic *homo sapiens,* and early *Homo sapiens sapiens.* It appears possibly to be an entirely different species on the basis of DNA studies. The species disappeared—possibly due to conflict with more modern man. The earlier *Homo erectus* were felt to definitely have speech, on the basis of imprints in the skull for Broca's speech area, and it is very possible that Neanderthals also had this faculty. The species buried its own dead often with apparent preparations for an afterlife.

5. *Homo sapiens sapiens.* Archaic specimens appeared to exist between 500,000 and 200,000 years ago. Modern man first appeared about 140,000 years ago. The average brain size is about 1350 cc.

The history of the hominids therefore extends over a period of about 4 million years. There undoubtedly has been a steady progression of intelligence and talents. Does it bear the hallmark of divine creation—could a god have used evolution as his means of fashioning a creature in his own image? It all seems painfully labored and fraught with so much suffering all along the way. Richard Dawkins, the English neo-Darwinian, feels there is clear-cut evidence of an *absence* of God, stating: "The universe we observe has precisely the properties we should expect if there is, at bottom, no design, no purpose, no evil and no good, nothing but blind, pitiless indifference." (Dawkins, 2006)

That is a daunting assessment. Is it, however, too premature and too superficial? There could be a plan; but it appears to have got out of synchronization! Could the genetic clock have slowed to an absurd pace due to its separation on our tiny far-flung planet from its essential cosmic origin and influence? That is a question we will return to in our final chapters.

DOES EVERYONE BELIEVE IN THIS CONCEPT OF THE EVOLUTION OF MAN?

It has been reported, on the basis of two polls conducted by ABC News and CBS News (2004), that:

- Fifty-five percent of Americans believe that God created humans in our present form.
- Twenty-seven per cent of Americans believe that humans evolved but that God guided the process.
- Thirteen percent believe that humans evolved without any guidance from God.

In Europe, belief in unguided evolution appears to be much higher and forty-eight percent of Britons feel that evolution is the best explanation for life's development.

Why do many lay people feel uncertain about the truth of evolution? That seems to settle around the following points:

- It may be a scientific paradigm which will eventually be disproved.
- The number of fossil bones, on which this theory is based, is relatively small.
- The radio-isotope dating techniques (radiocarbon up to 30 thousand years ago, and potassium-argon dating for volcanic rocks up to at least 2 million years) may prove to be unreliable.

However, most of the scientific world believes in human evolution under basically the plan outlined. It is generally accepted that hominid life originated in Africa from where it later spread (the "Out Of Africa" model). *Homo erectus* is felt to have left first over a million years ago followed later by *Homo sapiens*. There is also a "Multi Regional Model" whereby *Homo erectus* is felt to have given rise in multiple regions to *Homo Sapiens* in such widely dispersed locations as China, Indonesia, and even Europe.

How Do Our Two Primatologists Sum Up This Process?

Both writers are at pains to point out the higher qualities of the ape species that they have both studied. Here is a relevant quotation from De Wall:

> So much for the survival of the fittest. There is plenty of that, too, of course, but there is no need to caricature the life of our ape relatives as one led while constantly looking over their shoulders. Primates find great comfort in each other's company. Getting along with others is a critical skill because survival chances outside the groups, where there are predators and hostile neighbors, are dismal. Primates who find themselves alone meet a quick death. This explains why they spend an extraordinary amount of time servicing social ties as by grooming each other. (De Wall 2005)

With his discovery of reconciliation among primates, Dewall founded the field of animal conflict resolution studies. He comments very little in the

field of Religion there being only three brief tangential references in his recent book. On the other hand, Barbara King's whole book, in its 249 pages,
is preoccupied with the religious parallels of evolving primate social behavior and altruism—indeed the book is entitled *Evolving God*. She developed
the concept of the quality of belongingness which she defines as follows:

> Belongingness is mattering to somebody who matters to you. It's
> about getting positive feelings from our relationships...it extends to
> animals as well (other animals, for we humans are first and foremost
> animals). Relating emotionally to others shapes the very qualities of
> our lives. (King 2007)

She traces the origin of belongingness to behavior traits in the Great
Apes and carries on a concept of development through the various human
hominid stages. I will give her the final word in this debate:

> Yet the power of belongingness amounts to the power to base our
> lives, the lives of all humans who are intertwined in a globe-sized
> web of belongingness, on an understanding that we all come from
> the same roots. We evolved as primates; as ancestral hominids in
> Africa; as settlers of all the corners of our world; and finally as people
> who act in relation to sacred beings. We are primates still, able to
> embrace the expression of different faiths, or no faith at all, as we
> continue to make meaning through belongingness. (King 2007)

It is an endearing but unifying concept and we will explore it further
in a number of lives who have sought to express faith in a variety of ways.
Before that, however, we must examine the stance of the neuroscientist to
help us explore the anatomy and physiology of our evolved brain.

**Answer: A concept of belongingness may link us with our
simian forebears and enable us to discern meaning in that bond.**

Reading List and Sources
Our Inner Ape. Frans De Wall. Riverhead Books. Penguin Group. 2005.
Evolving God. Barbara King. Doubleday. 2007.

CHAPTER 8. NEUROSCIENTISTS SEEK THE POSSIBLE GOD SPOT IN THE HUMAN BRAIN

Paul Maclean and Michael Persinger

Question: Is there a mystical center or "God Spot" in the human brain to make a religious view on life meaningful?

WHO IS MICHAEL PERSINGER?

Michael Persinger is a university professor and cognitive neuroscience researcher working at the Laurentian University in Ontario Canada. Since 1971 he has built up a Behavioral Neuroscience Program focused around the influence of magnetic fields on brain activity. He obtained an M.A. in physiological psychology from the University of Tennessee and a Ph.D. from the University of Manitoba. The Laurentian University is situated somewhat off the normal beaten track being in the mining town of Sudbury north of Lake Huron. His work however is right on the main track of a new subject known as Neurotheology, which has brought him great interest and also a measure of controversy. This is particularly due to his claim that a weak magnetic field could stimulate part of the right temporal lobe to induce a mystical or religious state. The sensation was described as an "ethereal presence in the room end," which could be interpreted by significant numbers of his experimental subjects as the presence of God or in more general terms as a sensed presence. His findings on this and related topics have been the subject of over 200 published papers in professional journals.

Before considering Persinger's special contribution, it is relevant to set out some basic concepts of brain function already established:

PAUL MACLEAN AND THE TRIPLE BRAIN

The American neuro-anatomist and psychiatrist Paul MacLean, pioneered the idea that the human brain could be considered in three main parts or indeed as three brains on the basis of evolution:

1. The Reptilian Brain

The brain stem is the primitive early part of that structure and can be viewed as the automatic brain regulating basic functions and reflexes. It houses important parts of the reticular system which alerts the individual to danger. It is the source of rage and aggression as a response to that alerting. The crocodile in danger will exemplify this very basic, unsophisticated killer type of response.

2. The Mammalian Brain

With the advent of mammalian species, the limbic or emotional part of the brain started to develop prominently. Limbus means a margin and this new structure envelops the upper part of the brain stem. It houses such important structures as the amygdala (meaning an almond in view of its shape) governing basic emotion and the hippocampus (termed the seahorse again in view of its shape) which houses the memory components of emotion. The Limbic Brain enables the individual to bring feeling into his or her response to danger and pain. The young puppy, who is hurt, will exhibit whining and a sad expression if hurt particularly by its beloved owner. This will modulate the harsh aggression of the Reptilian Brain. It does however mediate the herd instinct as a response to perceived danger.

3. The Primate Cortical Brain

With the evolution of the Primates, leading to the eventual entry of man, there was a huge development of the cerebral hemispheres which brought in cognition and prior knowledge into a response to adverse stimuli.

MacLean points out that these three brains may not always act together in a coordinated and meaningful manner. Let me quote him: "We might imagine that when the psychiatrist bids the patient to lie on the couch, he is asking him to stretch out alongside a horse and a crocodile." (MacLean 1990)

The Reptilian Brain may be thought of as responsible for man's killer instincts when the cortical brain does not give adequate controlling influence. The Mammalian Brain may be responsible for the Herd instinct where man as an unthinking group may be capable of ostracism or destructive panic reactions. It is as though we made a car latching together three diverse engines hoping that it will always function smoothly and dependably.

Freud also had the model of a three part brain. The primitive reptilian brain he called the Id, the core part of the brain he termed the Ego. A higher component was the Super Ego which had the possibility of controlling the other two parts. This equated with the Conscience being a feeling of rightness for a particular action fashioned by parental and cultural influences.

4. The Executive Frontal Lobes

The Frontal Lobes of the brain have been called the Executive Brain. In formulating a plan of action, they allow the influence of two uniquely human contributions namely Prior Experience and also the Capability of Inhibition. This means that we can utilize past memories to guide us. We can decide not to follow the dictates of the vengeful reptilian brain or the herd instinct of the mammalian brain. Sadly we do not always utilize these moderating mechanisms to good effect!

• The Left Brain Versus Right Brain

We have two cerebral hemispheres each of which has a very different emphasis—this differentiation appears to have been made complete in the case of *Homo sapiens*. The left brain is the intellectually active hemisphere while the right brain is the holistic, reflective hemisphere. The left brain controls the dominant right arm which may hold the weapon whereas the right brain controls the left arm which cradles the baby. The two sides are united by the corpus callosum as a coordinating bridge-interestingly the female has more connecting fibers in the front part of the corpus than the male suggesting a greater integrative capacity. Data on respective roles of the two hemispheres has been forthcoming in so called "split brain" patients, who have had the corpus callosum divided usually as a treatment for uncontrollable epilepsy.

NEUROTHEOLOGY

Human groups throughout the world, from the earliest times, have exhibited four basic types of apparently instinctual activities:

• language

- music
- art
- religion

For the first three of these faculties there is an acknowledged special center in the brain namely a speech center, a hearing center, and a visual center, each with association tracts to neighboring parts of the brain. The details of each of these types of activity may vary greatly between races and geographical regions probably due to the extraordinary inventiveness of the human species. For example western and eastern music sound very different but may exhibit very basic patterns of harmony and even the concept of the octave.

Neurotheology sets out to explore whether the brain is equally hard-wired for mystical and religious experience. Such books as *Neurotheology: Brain, Science, Spirituality, Religious Experience*, edited and contributed to by R. Joseph (2003) and *Why God Won't Go Away* by Andrew Newberg and Eugene d'Aquili (2001) come to the basic conclusion that the human brain is so structured as to incorporate a religious sense, and that indeed this is a religious faculty which may have an evolutionary value in that it produces social cohesion and an increased survival rate. It is generally recognized that people with religious beliefs tend to live longer and happier lives in present day society, possibly because a lack of meaningfulness breeds depression and hopelessness. The big question is whether there is an actual mystical or religious center in the brain analogous to those for speech, hearing and sight. This postulated center has been nicknamed "the God Spot" and its most likely location is in the right temporo-parietal region. It is noteworthy that this is in the holistic creative right hemisphere. The evidence for this center comes particularly from the study of epileptic patients and the work of such researchers as Wilder Penfield and Michael Persinger in brain stimulation in this area.

Epilepsy (The Sacred Disease): Dostoevsky

Dostoevsky, the eminent 19th century Russian novelist, was himself epileptic and described the characteristics of his own condition in his celebrated novel *The Idiot*. Previously Hippocrates the 5th century B.C.E Father of Medicine, called epilepsy "the sacred disease" because certain patients in the preceding aura before a fit would experience very profound feelings and often a sense of being in touch with the Gods. Modern medicine recognizes that it is patients with so called temporal lobe epilepsy who are most likely to exhibit this. Let us quote Dostoevsky in his description of his own aura: "A feeling of reconciliation and of ecstatic devotional merging in the highest synthesis of life........that second really might be worth the whole of life." (Dostoevsky, 2004)

He indicated that at that moment the sufferer might feel that he or she had actually seen the Sensed Presence which they interpreted as God himself.

Wilder Penfield, the eminent Canadian neurosurgeon, had a special interest in seeking out an epileptic focus in order to excise it as part of the treatment of epilepsy. He would expose the whole side of the brain under local anesthesia in the conscious patient. Penfield would then carry out careful serial electrical stimulation to seek out the epileptic focus—such stimulation is painless. He made very detailed notes of patient's sensations during stimulation and indeed our knowledge of neurophysiology has been greatly enhanced by this work. In the right temporo-parietal region he would find that patients had most unusual experiences particularly a feeling of leaving the body or other mystical manifestations. It was from here that Persinger's work has stimulated the search for this mystical center and a study of its attributes.

PERSINGER'S WORK ON MAGNETIC STIMULATION OF THE BRAIN AND THE CONCEPT OF THE MYSTICAL CENTER

In approximately one thousand human subjects, Persinger has undertaken the application of very complex, weak magnetic fields which have the potential to interact with the subtle but complex neuro-electromagnetic processes associated with consciousness and the subtle nuances that define human experience. The very low frequency, very weak (similar to the intensity generated by a computer screen or hair dryer), complex magnetic fields applied through the temporo-parietal regions of the brain were selected because of their penetrability. Persinger claimed that a significant number of his subjects after stimulation experienced:

- out-of-body experiences
- unitive feelings with the cosmos
- a sensed presence

Persinger comments:

The results of these studies strongly suggested that the Sensed Presence, a phenomenon that had been the subject matter of paranormal experiences and mystical elaborations for millennia, could be evoked experimentally. The predominance of the experience during or just following stimulation of the right hemisphere was considered strong support, but not proof, that the sensed presence was the experience of the awareness of the right hemispheric equivalent of the left hemispheric sense of Self. (Persinger 2003)

Persinger suggests that intermittent shifts in the earth's magnetic field strengths have been shown to decrease nocturnal melatonin levels and to increase the circulating levels of the epileptogenic neuropeptide CRF (corticotrophin releasing factor). This would explain the greater occurrence of a sensed presence and apparitions during the early morning hours and also at times of increased geomagnetic activity in the earth's magnetic field strength.

THE SIGNIFICANCE OF THESE FINDINGS FOR MAN'S RELIGIOUS OR MYSTICAL FACULTY

Persinger found that he could identify individuals particularly prone to spontaneous activity of this center by using his own Personal Philosophy Inventory or the Robert's Inventory for epileptic spectrum disorder.

The correlation coefficients between the number of different paranormal experiences and scores for temporal lobe sensitivity, as inferred from responses to clusters of items from these inventories, ranged between 0.5 and 0.9. The individuals who had elevated scores for these inventories were also found to show more prominent alpha rhythms on electroencephalography over the temporal lobes. These forms of spontaneous activity he termed Temporal Lobe Transients (TLTs).

Interestingly, Persinger equated the tendency for TLTs to those who were "Introspectives." This tendency was often related to high creative activity. The list of such susceptible subjects was:

- writers
- artists
- musicians
- women
- older people.

I have a favorite painting in mind of the poet John Keats involved in creative activity as evidenced by an open book and a pen on his lap. In the painting, by Joseph Severn, he holds his hand over the right parietal region as if to encourage the creative muse! Keats qualified as a doctor in England but had to give up his practice because of the devastating effect on his sensitive nature of seeing operations in 19th century hospitals carried out without anesthesia (similar to the experiences of Charles Darwin). One of his greatest works is entitled *La Belle Dame Sans Merci*, in which he describes what could be called a Sensed Presence of an almost goddess-like figure coming into his consciousness. Keats described life thus: "Life is a Vale of Soul Making." (Keats's Letters)

His talent was cut short at the age of 26, when he died from tuberculosis, a disease which had claimed so many of his family.

WHAT IS THE SIGNIFICANCE OF A MYSTICAL CENTER(S) IN THE BRAIN?

If we do have a mystical center or centers in our brain, that is we are wired for mysticism, it could help us to provide the fortitude and faith to survive the "slings and arrows of outrageous fortune" (to use Hamlet's phraseology)! It must be noted that Persinger himself is an Agnostic although ascribing a great significance to his findings in influencing human conduct. A joint study by two Swedish universities found difficulties in replicating Persinger's findings using the identical magnetic field apparatus and 89 students in psychology and theology. There were however reported experiences in both the test and control group subjects who were highly suggestible (as determined by the use of a special questionnaire). It has been pointed out that Persinger's studies were not double blinded. Clearly much more work needs to be carried out in this field although the work from epileptic subjects alone substantiates Persinger's hypothesis. Let us end with another quotation from Persinger: "The power of the God Experience shames any known therapy. With a single burst in the temporal lobe, people find structure and meaning in seconds. With it come the personal conviction of truth and the sense of self selection." (Persinger, 2003)

Mario Beauregard, another neuroscientist, and Denyse O'Leary in their non-reductionist 2007 book *The Spiritual Brain* deny a single god spot pointing to a whole complex of centers, including the right parietal regions, observed by them to come into play on functional MRI in mystical meditation on God by Carmelite nuns:

> This state was associated with significant loci of activation in the right medial orbitofrontal cortex, right middle temporal cortex, right inferior and superior parietal lobules, right caudate ,left medial prefrontal cortex, left anterior cingulated cortex, left inferior pari-

etal lobule, left insula, left caudate, and left brain stem Other loci of activation were seen in the extra-striate visual cortex. These results suggest that mystical experiences are mediated by several brain regions and systems. (Beauregard and O'Leary 2007)

The authors believe in the authenticity of mystical experiences as a direct link with a supernatural sphere differing from Persinger's agnosticism. It is a fascinating debate. The complexity of the brain's processing in this aspect should come as no surprise. I am mindful, in my own medical sphere, of the search for an isolated pain center in the nervous system, which was followed by the discovery on the basis of modern imaging studies that pain is processed in multiple integrated centers. Such is the subtlety of design, whatever its origin, in the brain.

> Answer: Evidence for a system of mystical processing
> mechanisms in the brain offers a meaningful link between
> all the world's religions, both theistic and non-theistic.

Reading List and Sources

The Neurophysiology of Paranormal Experiences. Journal of Neuropsychiatry and Clinical Neurosciences. Michael Persinger. 2001. 13:4. P. 515-5

The Triune Brain in Evolution. PD Mac Lean. Plenum. 1990.

The Spiritual Brain. Mario Beauregard and Denyse O'Leary. Harper One 2007

CHAPTER 9. THE UNIFAITH STANCE

Pierre Teilhard De Chardin and Francis Collins

Question: If we believe that there is only one true religion, will this give us a unique sense of meaning?

THE CHOICE OF BEING RELIGIOUS: PIERRE TEILHARD DE CHARDIN

Even in the Existentialist or Post Modern world view, where there is no ultimate meaning, the individual may choose a religious stance in the world. Pierre Teilhard De Chardin made such a choice in a totally uncompromising and original way. He was born in 1881 in the town of Orcines, in France, to a pious Catholic family. The tag of De Chardin is a vestige of a French aristocratic title. His regard for nature obviously came from his father who was a keen amateur naturalist invoking in the young boy an interest in collecting such items as insects, stones, and samples of plant life. The spiritual side of his nature appeared to have been instilled by his mother. He was ordained as a Jesuit priest. In addition to his religious studies, Teilhard was educated in mathematics, geology, and biology. This gave him a unique combination of being a man of the spirit and a man of nature. This conditioned his very special viewpoint on life but it was a stance which did not always endear him to his church superiors and sadly much of his work was denied publication during his lifetime by the Roman Holy Office.

An Unmatched Experience of the World

The Church was often uncertain how best to employ Teilhard's talents, so that they allowed him to develop his biological interests often in far flung parts of the world. He worked initially in the paleontology laboratory of the French Museum of Natural History in Paris. He later studied under Professor Marcellin Boulle, who was an authority in human paleontology particularly of the Neanderthal period introducing Teilhard to the subject of human evolution. He encountered the works of the French philosopher Henri Bergson: his book *Creative Evolution* was particularly influential. This expounded the view that Evolution results from a life force (élan vital) which is creative although frequently unpredictable in its effects. Teilhard traveled the western and eastern world in his paleontolological studies and worked particularly in Egypt, China, and India. He became friends with another churchman with archaeological interests, the Abbé Henri Breuil. Breuil was perhaps the greatest authority on Paleolithic cave art. Together they studied the caves of northern Spain and France.

War Service and an Experience of Evil

Teilhard's studies were interrupted when he was conscripted in December 1914 during World War I as a stretcher bearer in the 8th regiment of Moroccan rifle men. He served with great valor in the trenches where he was aware of the pointless death of countless thousands of young men under appalling conditions. He served with little concern for his own personal safety so that he was awarded the Médaille Militaire and the Legion of Honor. He summed this up subsequently as "meeting with the Absolute." He commented on evil in his final great work, *The Phenomenon of Man*:

> If we regard the march of the world from the standpoint of its risks and the efforts it requires, we soon see, under the veil of security and harmony which, viewed from on high envelop the rise of man, a particular type of cosmos in which evil appears necessary and abundantly as you like in the course of evolution—not by accident (which would not much matter) but through the very structure of the system. (De Chardin, 1959)

The Central Place of Evolution

Teilhard became involved in many sites of excavation of hominid remains throughout the world. Most important of these was his major role in China in the discovery of Peking Man now recognized as a form of *Homo erectus*, who Teilhard felt to have been the first human precursor to use advanced forms of hand tools and have the mastery of fire. He embraced Evolution as the key to what he saw as God's intended pathway for nature and man. His geological knowledge made him aware of the timescale of the earth being in thousands of millions of years as opposed to Archbishop Usher's seventeenth century date for the Creation of 4004 BC. The Catholic Church was not ready for this radical point of view which it saw as a dangerous threat to biblical Creationism as exhibited in Genesis and ideas of Original Sin requiring the concept of a Garden of Eden. This meant that his last great book *The Phenomena of Man*, where he expounds his views on evolution could not be published until after his death. In that work he sums up the purposive nature of evolution:

> We have seen and admitted that evolution is an ascent toward consciousness. That is no longer contested even by the most materialistic or at all events by the most agnostic of humanitarians. Therefore it should culminate forwards in some sort of supreme consciousness. (De Chardin 1959)

The Thinking Noosphere

Teilhard was able to see life in all its perspective, which he commented upon, saying, "If we look far enough back in the depths of time, the disordered anthill of living beings suddenly, for an informed observer, arranges itself in long files that make their way by various paths towards greater consciousness." (De Chardin, 1959)

Teilhard's vision saw a progression of stages:

- Geogenesis—the evolution of the earth itself.
- Biogenesis—the evolution of living creatures.
- Noogenesis—the evolution of mind (from the Greek word "noos," for "mind".)

He comments, "And this amounts to imagining, in one way or another, above the animal biosphere a human sphere, a sphere of reflection, of conscious invention, of conscious souls (the noosphere, if you will)." (De Chardin 1959)

Father of the World Wide Web

Teilhard felt that we, as thinking beings, are being brought closer and closer by an ever tightening network of consciousness—the Thinking Noosphere. In his time, he had in mind libraries, museums, the media, the radio, and the advent of television. He died in 1955 and was therefore unaware of the development of the Internet, though one can almost hear him murmuring now, "Mon Dieu! That is exactly what I was telling you about!"

He fell, in recent years, somewhat into obscurity, although this is quite unjustified. However, he is now being hailed as the Father of the World

Wide Web. There is no doubt that we are now in an era of a universal consciousness. For example, television and the Internet can make us aware of any world event as it is happening—we can survey the view from a tank in Iraq and judge events from minute to minute. We have the choice to react, take action, ignore what we see and hear but there is a possibility of total awareness and universalized cerebration.

Finding a Cosmic Viewpoint

Teilhard's all embracing vision allowed him to see beyond the confines of this planet to our developing knowledge and consciousness of the great Cosmos beyond. Our planet is but one amongst a host of others in our Galaxy, the Milky Way. Our galaxy itself is one amongst perhaps 50 billion others. Teilhard was very well aware of this and felt passionately that our vision of ourselves should be cosmic.

The Need for an Omega Point

In all of this revolutionary environment, Teilhard felt that there was an urgent need for mankind to come together and be able to focus and agree upon a common point which he called the Omega Point. He saw life as being a religious experience as expounded in his great book *The Divine Milieu*. From his own viewpoint, he saw the omega point as being Christ. Furthermore he conceived it as the Cosmic Christ whose presence permeated the farthest reaches of the Universe. It may be however, in the current era, we will need a more universalistic focus which allows people of all faiths to participate in its vision and that we will explore in further chapters.

The Future of Man and the Phenomenon of Man

These are the titles of Teilhard's two great books in which he expounds his vision of man's possibility for transcendence but also his greatest hazard if he cannot come together as a species with an agreed consensus. This is indeed a sobering thought. What will it take to make us all as one? If conscious life is indeed discovered eventually on some other planet in the Universe, then indeed the inhabitants of this planet may have to find a sense of common identity and pride to meet the supreme challenge of confronting another civilization which could be very different from our own in its state of development and its spiritual life. We should indeed be grateful to Teilhard for his vision which alerts us to that challenge.

FRANCIS COLLINS, ANOTHER SCIENTIST WITH A UNIFAITH VIEW

Francis Collins has recently declared his strong beliefs as a Christian expounded particularly in his recent book *The Language of God. A Scientist Presents Evidence for Belief*, published in 2006. Collins is a very eminent scientist being one of the world's leading geneticists and the long time head of the Human Genome Project. The cover of his book shows a DNA spiral portrayed as a stained glass window in a church obviously attributing its existence to God. Collins initially undertook a Ph.D. program in physical chemistry at Yale and then felt the vocation to undertake also a medical degree in the University of North Carolina. He relates: "Within a few weeks I knew medical school was the right place for me. I loved the intellectual stimulation, the ethical challenges, the human element and the amazing complexity of the human body." (Collins, 2006)

As a medical student he undertook a course on medical genetics which intrigued him providing him with the vocation to help those afflicted by genetic disease. After qualifying he sought to train himself in the exacting techniques of DNA sequencing. He helped to discover the genetic misspellings in such incapacitating diseases as cystic fibrosis, neurofibromatosis and Huntingdon's disease. He was then appointed to the challenging post of head of the Human Genome Project based in Washington. This set out to crack the human genetic code and was successful at the beginning of this new millennium. The Human Genome consists of all the DNA of our species, the hereditary code of life. Collins explained that the newly discovered text "...was 3 billion letters long and written in a strange and cryptographic four-letter code. Such is the amazing complexity of the information carried within each cell of the human body, that a live reading of that code at a rate of one letter per second would take thirty one years, even if reading continued day and night." (Collins, 2006)

After a decade of intense effort with his team, Collins found himself standing beside President Bill Clinton in the East Room of the White House, along with Craig Venter, the leader of a competing private sector genetic enterprise. Announcing to the world on television this tremendous discovery. President Clinton said on that occasion:

> Without a doubt, this is the most important, most wondrous map ever produced by human kind. Today, we are learning the language in which God created life. We are gaining ever more awe for the

complexity, the beauty and the wonder of God's most divine and sacred gift. (Clinton, 2000)

Collins agreed with the President's sentiments but he had not always been a Christian. His parents were free thinkers and Collins was initially an agnostic. He later became an atheist—he states that sixty percent of scientists in the USA are atheists. In all truth however, he had not really had the time to make a considered opinion on this matter. He was challenged by a patient who asked him whether he was a believer; the patient had great faith which was helping her obviously to face an incurable disease in her mind. This piercing question caused Francis Collins to go through a period of self appraisal. A book which helped him greatly was *Mere Christianity* by C.S. Lewis, a celebrated Oxford academic, who had himself initially been an atheist.

The Importance of the Moral Code

The factor that was central to Collins conversion was his sudden realization of the importance of the moral law within us. He explains:

> What we have here is very peculiar: the concept of right and wrong appears to be universal among all members of the human species (though its application may result in wildly different outcomes). It thus seems to be a phenomenon approaching that of a law, like the law of gravitation or of special relativity. As best as I can tell, this law appears to apply peculiarly to human beings. (Collins, 2006)

Collins comments that other animals may at times appear to show glimmerings of a moral sense, but they are certainly not wide spread. In many instances other species' behavior seems to be in dramatic contrast to any sense of universal rightness. He cites examples of the moral law as follows:

1. The Altruistic Impulse

2. The Voice of Conscience calling us to help others even if nothing is received in return.

3. The Pang of Conscience that is felt after committing a falsehood.

Collins was led to consider the fact that human beings can be loving creatures. He classified love into four progressive grades namely agape (selfless love), affection, friendship and lastly romantic love. He felt strongly that Agape could not have arisen by the blindly operating processes of Darwinian natural selection but pointed strongly to the presence of a loving God. Strangely, Collins does not agree with the current school of Intelligent

Design feeling that the inherent properties of the genome are sufficient to explain all of evolution.

A DIALOGUE BETWEEN DE CHARDIN AND COLLINS

Both of these eminent scientists undertake the Unifaith Stance: one was a Catholic and the other is a Protestant but both are in the Christian tradition. Both would agree that evolution as now conceived by modern science is God's way of producing the living world. Both would agree that it should produce a startling expansion of human consciousness transforming the world. Teilhard De Chardin was particularly aware of the implications for this for the Macrocosm in the form of the Cosmos. Francis Collins is particularly focused on the Microcosm with the ever widening possibilities for the human genome. The presence of the moral code gives him some measure of confidence in man's developing spiritual consciousness. One is reminded of the celebrated saying of the German philosopher Immanuel Kant of the 18th Century on these two facets: "Two things fill the mind with ever new and increasing admiration and awe—the starry heavens above and the moral law within." (Kant, 1785)

Kant was credited with uniting the two major trends of philosophy of his age, namely Empiricism and Rationalism. Empiricism emphasizes the all importance of outside sensory data while rationalism relies on the innate properties of the human mind. In this sense, De Chardin and Collins can also be seen to unite these two viewpoints each of them the combination of a scientist and a mystic. It is interesting that Collins announced (2008) his intention to step down from the Human Genome Project to devote himself to writing—however President Obama has recently appointed him as Director of the National Institute of Health (August 17th 2009).He will be an inspired choice, but we may have to wait a little longer for his next book! We have seen that a discovery of Evolution drove Darwin to be an Agnostic and Behe to question the existence of a loving God whereas Chardin and Collins saw it as a revelation of their God's way of development of life.

Answer: Certainly the consciousness of a
single true faith is supremely significant to these two
remarkable thinkers, but unfortunately a Unifaith stance
tends to divide mankind on the basis of belief.

Reading List and Sources

The Phenomenon of Man. Teilhard De Chardin. Fontana Religious Books 1965.

The Language of God. A Scientist Presents Evidence for Belief. Francis Collins. Free Press 2006.

CHAPTER 10. INTERFAITH: JOHN HICK AND THE DALAI LAMA

> Question: Is it possible to identify the common
> points of the World's Religion in order to allow
> a meaningful dialogue between them?

THE LIMITATIONS OF A UNIFAITH VIEWPOINT

The subjects of our previous chapter, Teilhard De Chardin and Francis Collins, had an exclusively Unifaith attitude to religion. Teilhard De Chardin felt that the world needed to agree on a single Omega Point namely that of Christianity with a Cosmic Christ centrally placed there. Although always charitable in his disposition, he was dismissive of the religions of the East such as Hinduism and Buddhism and particularly to the primal faiths which he saw exhibited in the great cave paintings of the Upper Paleolithic periods in southern France and Spain. He regarded the latter as an evolutionary form of religion only. However, we now live in a world where the major World Religions start to interface with each other—in any large western city they will all be represented. Should each one see itself in an exclusivist position with regard to the others? Alternatively, do they each have something to say to the others and should the others be willing and interested to listen?

WHO IS JOHN HICK?

Professor John Hick is someone who has taken this problem as the center point of his life's work and endeavor. He was born in 1922 but is still very active in his eighties. He had wished to prepare for the Presbyterian ministry but decided to take a preliminary four year honors course in philosophy in the University of Edinburgh (where I undertook my Certificate course). He subsequently carried out two years research at Oriel College Oxford and then undertook his first teaching post in the philosophy department at Cornell University in the USA. All of this training enabled him to speak as both a theologian and a philosopher. His senior academic posts were as Professor of Theology at Birmingham University in England (my home city) and as Danforth Professor of Religion at Claremont Graduate School, in California. It is important to note however that before taking these senior posts he served as an ordinary Presbyterian Minister at Belford in Northumberland in the north of England. This can be seen to account for his straightforward "feet on the ground" attitude to today's problems. He soon became interested in the interrelationship of the world's great religions and this has been the particular thrust of his life's work.

The Concept of Plurality

Hick developed a pluralist view to the world religions as opposed to an exclusivist one as taken up by Teilhard De Chardin and Francis Collins. He expounded this particularly in his book *God and the Universe of Faiths* in 1973. Although he identified himself as a Christian with Buddhist leanings, he did not agree that Christ should be the central or Omega Point. He felt initially that God should be at the center with all of the World Faiths grouped around that central focus. He saw this as a Copernican View of religion similar to that which occurred in astronomy when the sun was realized to be the center of the planetary system (Heliocentric) rather than the earth (Geocentric) as envisaged in the Ptolemaic viewpoint generally held prior to the 16th century. In his choice of this sort of metaphor, he was undoubtedly aware of the suppressive attitude of the Catholic Church to the Heliocentric view which had led, amongst other things, to the imprisonment of Galileo. A compromise position has been reached by the Catholic theologian Karl Rahner, who has presented an inclusive viewpoint whereby Christ did function in the other world religions whether their participants were aware of this or not. Hick did not agree with this inclusivist vision, feeling that it was demeaning to the other world religions implying that there was superiority in Christianity. Another Theologian, Raymond Panniker has spoken of a "hidden Christ" in the other faiths but again this was an unacceptable compromise to Hick.

A Question of Imaging the Transcendent: The Personae and the Impersonae of The Real

Hick began to realize that in order to include the non theistic religions such as Buddhism, Advaitic Hinduism, Jainism, Taoism, Confucianism, and Shinto he would have to substitute for the word God another term such as the Transcendent or the Real or the Noumen. He finally chose the term, the Real to give expression to the underlying focus in life. This could be expressed as a variety of human anthropomorphic forms who he called the Personae of the Real or as non-anthropomorphic forms which he termed the Impersonae.

Examples of the Personae would be:
- Jahweh or Jehovah in Judaism.
- The Holy Father in Christianity.
- Allah in Islam.
- Ahura Mazda in Zoroastrianism.
- Vishnu and Shiva in Hinduism.

Examples of the Impersonae would be:
- Brahman, the World Spirit in Advaitic Hinduism.
- Nirvana in Theravada Buddhism.
- Sunyata in Mahayana Buddhism.
- The Tao in Taoism.
- The Way of Heaven in Confucianism.
- The Kami of Shinto.
- The Path of the Ford Makers in Jainism.

This viewpoint was clearly and exhaustively presented in Hick's greatest book *An Interpretation of Religion. Human Responses to the Transcendent.* published in 1989. This was an expanded version of his 1986 to 1987 Gifford lectures delivered in the University of Edinburgh. This is a wonderful and healing work, which holds out metaphorical arms to all those in the world who embrace a religion of any sort. It invites them all in to contribute to a dialogue in which all are important and none is subservient. This is Hicks great contribution to Theology and Philosophy and a message that is surely essential for the 21st century if we are to prevent religious conflict from enveloping the world in a disastrous manner.

Hick summarized the 3 common points of the world's great rligions as:

1. They all have a Cosmic Optimism: "All will ultimately be well".

2. The Golden Rule is Central: "Do unto others as you would be done by".

3. A Change from Self Centeredness to Reality Centeredness is the essential conversion.

I have found these common points enormously helpful in contemplating the sometimes bewildering variety of the world's faiths.

The Golden Rule embraces:

- Compassion
- Koruna
- Agape

It is surely the core of religion when the surrounding myth and magic are shed.

Reaction of the Official Church to Hick's Concept of Plurality

The classic view of the Roman Catholic Church was a totally exclusivist one employing the Latin phrase, *Extra ecclesiam nulla salus.* (Vatican II 1979) This is translated as "outside the Roman Catholic Church there is no salvation." However, documents issued after Vatican II (1963–1965) together with the papal statement Redemptor Hominis (1979) showed a much-changed attitude indicating that non-Christians do receive the grace of God and are united with Christ in a manner which, though mysterious and known only to God, truly saves. This can be taken to be the view of the Pope at that time, John Paul II. In 1996, however, Pope John Paul II delegated Cardinal Ratzinger, Prefect of the Congregation for the Doctrine of the Faith (formally known as the Holy Inquisition) to address a group of 80 Catholic bishops about the central threats to the Christian faith, which at that time were specifically seen as pluralism and relativism. John Hick was referred to as a central figure in this controversy. Cardinal Ratzinger summed up his attitude as follows:

> In the end, for Hick, religion means that man goes from "self-centeredness" as the systems of the old Adam, to "reality-centeredness" as existence of the new man, thus extending from one's self to the otherness of one's neighbor. It sounds beautiful, but when it is considered in depth it appears as empty and vacuous as the call to authenticity by Bultmann, who in turn has taken the concept from Heidegger. For this, religion is not necessary. (Ratzinger 1996)

We must be aware of course, of course, that Cardinal Ratzinger is now the Pope and is becoming known for his uncompromising and fundamentalist viewpoint.

The Interfaith Movement and the World Congress of Faiths

John Hick's work has been undertaken in a very seminal time in which the concept of Interfaith Dialogue has presented itself. Hick's ideas are entirely in conformity with this movement as we may see from the following quotation:

> The great world religions then, I suggest, constitute different ways of conceiving and therefore different ways of experiencing, and therefore different ways of responding in life to the ultimate eternal and ineffable reality; and so far as we can tell from their fruits in human life, they are more or less equally authentic. (Hick 1989)

Hick felt that Christianity's viewpoint that Christ was God incarnate was an exclusivist claim which hindered dialogue with the other world religions. He edited a very controversial anthology entitled *The Myth of God Incarnate* and a personal book *The Metaphor of God Incarnate*. He points out that study of the historical Jesus makes it unlikely that Jesus did in fact claim to be God by referring to himself as either "The Son of Man" or "The Son of God." Hick claimed that it was conventional in the first century for Jewish Teachers to refer to themselves as a Son of God without inferring biological parenthood. Of course, Cardinal Ratzinger in his previously mentioned dialogue found this viewpoint totally unacceptable.

The World Congress of Faiths was founded in London in 1936 by the explorer and mystic Sir Francis Younghusband. In 1936 London, the city of its origin, was capital of a multi-religious empire. Now London, like all the world's great cities, has become a multi-religious environment in a commonwealth of nations. Against this background, most major cities have Interfaith Associations where members of different religious persuasions meet together and exchange insights.

I participated in one of the annual pilgrimages of the Westminster Interfaith Group in 1994, and a group of about 400 people walked together for about twelve hours from southeast London to northwest London. These were some of the places we visited:

- A Sikh Gurdwara in Bow
- East London Mosque
- Bevis Marks Synagogue
- Saint Peter's Church
- Rigpa Tibetan Buddhist Center
- Upper Holloway Baptist Church

- Sanatan Hindu Mandir
- Rosslyn Hill Unitarian Chapel
- Hampstead Quakers Friends' House
- Zoroastrian House

At each of these centers, we were greeted by members of their congregation who welcomed us and sought to explain their religious viewpoint. We were offered refreshment and sincere greetings. Our guide and leader was Brother Daniel Faivre, a Catholic monk of saintly disposition with the ability to gather people around him and relate to them in a humorous and loving way. John Hick would definitely have approved.

The Interfaith movement sets out to encourage dialogue between the world's faiths. However, it advises that one keep one's own faith intact in this exchange. In the next chapter, we will examine the life of Gandhi, who set out himself to embrace multiple faiths and this is another great adventure.

THE DALAI LAMA

The Dalai Lama is an extraordinarily charismatic figure on the world stage linking east with west. He shares with John Hick the three concepts:

- The equal value of each of the world religions with each providing a special insight.
- The importance of keeping one's own religion intact and being observant against the background of the other faiths, in which one takes a deep interest.
- A strong sense of humor and equanimity amidst all the world's multiple troubles.

The Dalai Lama's Extraordinary Life

His life has a fairy tale aspect to it, a sort of "rags to riches" feel. He was born in 1935 as the fifth of sixteen children of an obscure farmer, of very modest means, in the far away northeastern part of Tibet, in the province of Ando. He was almost certainly destined to be a monk in a remote monastery in that area—he still calls himself merely a "humble monk." In this environment, he was spotted by a search team sent from the royal palace of Potala in the Tibetan capital of Lhasa on a mission to find the reincarnation of the thirteenth Dalai Lama. At the age of four years, he and his family were taken on a journey to Lhasa, taking four months, to change their whole lives in order that he might be trained to be the spiritual leader and also main temporal leader of the Tibetan people. It is the complete obverse of the story of his spiritual icon, the Buddha, who is said to have left the luxuries of a royal palace to become a wondering ascetic and eventually monk with his own following. He explains the circumstances in his autobiography entitled *Freedom in Exile* as follows:

> Now in my own case, I am held to be the reincarnation of each of the previous thirteen Dalai Lamas of Tibet (the first having been born in thirteen fifty one AD), who are in turn considered to be manifestations of Avalokiteshvara, or Chenrezig in Tibetan, Bodhisattva of Compassion, holder of the White Lotus. Thus I am believed also to be a manifestation of Chenrezig, in fact the seventy-fourth in a lineage that can be traced back to a Brahmin boy who lived in the time of the original Buddha Shakyamuni. I am often asked whether I truly believe this. The answer is not simple to give. But as a fifty-six year old, when I consider my experiences during this present life, and given my Buddhist beliefs, I have no difficulty accepting that I am spiritually connected both to the thirteen previous Dalai Lama's, to Chenrezig and to the Buddha himself. (Dalai Lama 1990)

The Dalai Lama states that when he visited two of the monasteries in Lhasa, they both seemed very familiar to him although he had never been there before. He became convinced of some connection from his previous lives. His early education was undertaken in the beautiful but austere surroundings of the Potala Palace built on a rocky outcrop known as the "Red Hill," in Lhasa. It was a lonely existence, at first with his brother, but later on a one to one basis with his tutors. He was enthroned at the early age of fifteen as Dalai Lama and Tibet's Head of State. He later undertook studies within a monastic environment for the Lharanga degree, which is effectively a doctorate in Buddhist philosophy. His curriculum embraced five major subjects being logic, Tibetan art and culture, Sanskrit, medicine and Buddhist philosophy. His five minor subjects were poetry, music and drama, astrology, meter and phrasing, and synonyms. He comments frankly that it was a very unbalanced and in many ways totally inappropriate course for the leader of a country during the late twentieth century. His mental resources from this rather closeted education were to be tested to the utmost. In 1959 Tibet was occupied by the forces of People's Republic of China after the collapse of Tibetan Resistance—he was then only twenty four. He had little alternative but to flee to northwest India in Dharamasala where he formed the Central Tibetan Administration (the Tibetan government in exile). In this life of reversals, he may well have reflected on the four central virtues of his faith of Buddhism:

- Benevolence
- Compassion
- Joy in the Joy of Others
- Equanimity

He has never lost his equanimity despite having to contemplate the violation of Tibet with the destruction of many of his beloved monasteries and the murder of large numbers of Buddhist monks and lamas. His attitude to China has always been one of restraint desiring a shared responsibility for Tibet combined with repair when many thought that he should express violent outrage and a call for revenge. His attitude and endless advocacy of peace in the world led to the award of the Nobel Peace Prize in 1989.

His comments about the Chinese are moderate; the following is typical: "The Communist Chinese are against religion in general and Buddhism in particular. They denounce religion as a poison, claiming that it harms economic growth and is a tool of exploitation. They even say that religion is an empty and meaningless pursuit." (Dalai Lama 1990.)

He states that Tibetans, on the other hand, believe in the Buddha's teaching and see it as a source of peace and happiness. Broadly speaking, he comments, Tibetans are indeed happy, peaceful, and resilient in the face of difficulties. Those who oppose religion tend to be more anxious and narrow-minded. He has noticed that Tibetans do well without having to work so hard while the Chinese struggle much harder to survive.

A Wish for Harmony among Religions

The Dalai Lama has constantly made a plea for harmony and mutual understanding between the World Religions. He has suggested that this may be promoted in the following ways:

- Meetings amongst scholars from different religious backgrounds in order to promote empathy and to improve knowledge about one another.
- To emphasize that the purpose of the major religious traditions is not to construct big temples on the outside, but to create temples of goodness and compassion inside in our hearts.
- To encourage the leaders of the world religions to come together to meet and to learn to pray together. He quotes the occasion of Assisi in 1986 when this happened on World Peace Day.

• For people of different religious traditions to go on pilgrimages to-gether to visit one another's holy places.

• To learn to meditate on the question of harmony.

The Dalai Lama has himself set an example in all of these matters. He has traveled to such pilgrimage centers as Lourdes and Jerusalem where he prayed with the followers of other religions sometimes "in silent med-itation." He records that in this prayer and meditation, he felt a genuine spiritual experience. In a unique manner for any major religious leader, he has gone out of his way to enter into dialogues with leaders of other world faiths. For example in a meeting organized by the World Community for Christian Meditation he made a detailed analogy between the teachings of Christ and the Buddha on the subject of compassion and forgiveness of one's enemies. He summarizes some of his feelings as follows:

> In order to develop a genuine spirit of harmony from a sound foun-dation of knowledge, I believe it is very important to know the fun-damental differences between religious traditions. And it is possible to understand the fundamental differences, but at the same time recognize the value and potential of each religious tradition. In this way, a person may develop a balanced and harmonious perception. Some people believe that the most reasonable way to attain harmony and solve problems relating to religious intolerance is to establish one universal religion for everyone. However I have always felt that we should have different religious traditions because human beings possess so many different mental dispositions. One religion simply cannot satisfy the needs of such a variety of people. If we tried to unify the faiths of the world into one religion, we will also lose many of the qualities and richness's of each particular tradition. Therefore, I feel it is better, in spite of the many quarrels in the name of religion, to maintain a variety of religious traditions." (Mehrota, *Essential Dalai Lama* 2005)

ACCORD BETWEEN JOHN HICK AND THE DALAI LAMA

Both of these men have given their lives to stressing the plurality of the world's religions and their cardinal value in life. John Hick has called himself a Christian with Buddhist leanings and the Dalai Lama has dem-onstrated by his actions that he is a Buddhist with Christian leanings. But their vision goes much further than that embracing the totality of man's religious background. John Hick comes from a theistic background whereas the Dalai Lama comes from a non-theistic background and yet they have so much common ground. John Hick is the academic whose thought and study has produced an intellectually satisfying basis for dialogue between the faiths of the world whether they are theistic or non-theistic on a basis of equal value but different insights. The Dalai Lama, on the other hand, has gone out onto the world stage as an ambassador for these sentiments rather than appealing to a more limited academic circle. Both men have written persuasively on the subject. The Dalai Lama's many books have the common touch being directed to the man in the street whereas John Hick has a more restricted but influential appeal to the intellectual. It is interesting that both of them stress that the individual should in general stay with his own faith strengthened by his knowledge of other traditions. Neither of them is tempted to advise change unless one finds that one's own faith does not meet one's needs. We will examine in the next chapter the attitude which allows an individual to branch out into other faiths and take them on together with his or her own background religion. This is exemplified by the life of Gandhi. All three of these men have a saintly disposition and the world has much to thank them for their example.

Answer: John Hick's common points allow a meaningful framework for much needed Interfaith discussion and worship but must we be limited to our one faith?

Reading List and Sources

An Interpretation of Religion. John Hick: Macmillan: London 1989 and New Haven: Yale University Press revised edition 2004

The Essential Dalai Lama. His Important Teachings. Edited by Rajiv Mehrota. Viking Press (Penguin Group) 2005.

CHAPTER 11. MULTIFAITH

Mahatma Gandhi And Wayne Teasdale
Question: Is it possible to practice more than one faith with increased meaning in our life?

Gandhi passionately believed that it was possible to embrace more than one faith or religion at the same time, as exemplified by his famous saying: "I am a Hindu, a Christian, a Muslim and a Jew." (Gandhi. *Essential Writings*, 1991)

We may note that this is different from the Interfaith attitude where one is advised to stay with one's own faith while at the same having a dialogue with others. Certainly the knowledge and texts of all the world's religions and philosophies are available in any modern city in its libraries and via the Internet. If we have made the decision as a person to regard life in a religious way can we look at the different alternative faiths as modules which can be latched together into a personal faith matrix? Or is that a heresy? Anyway, what is heresy in a multifaith context?

WHO WAS GANDHI?

Mohandas Karamchand Gandhi was born into a Hindu family at Porbander in Gujarat in India in 1869. From his own account, he was a lonely, unsure child who did not do well at school or college. His family managed to find the finance to enable him to go to London to undertake a three-year course in law, which gave him the status of a barrister. It was a very difficult time for him going from a rural background into the sophisticated environment of England's capital city, where he experienced racial prejudice for the first time. He passed his examinations and returned to India, but found himself unable to establish a legal practice there. An opportunity came for him to go to South Africa, but his initial attempts to establish himself were no more successful in that environment. He had to learn many new things such as bookkeeping, and he had to establish confidence and, most important, obtain a personal involvement with his clients who were Indic in background. Eventually he achieved a significant degree of success and was able to bring from India his faithful wife, Kasturbai, and his two children. Paradoxically, he started to become uneasy about his developing material prosperity, eventually giving away much of the material possessions of the family to good causes. Kasturbai was even asked to relinquish a diamond necklace that she had been given, which was one of many difficult sacrifices she was asked to undertake. The marriage often proved stormy due to Gandhi's unworldly selflessness.

Gandhi was concerned about racial prejudice, in particular as practiced by south Africa's white government in the Transvaal that introduced new legislation to deprive South African Indians of what civil rights they still retained (the so called "Black Act"). He developed the concept of civil disobedience and persuaded his fellow countrymen to take this up with eventual great effect. He stated: "Civil disobedience is the inherent right of a citizen. He dare not give it up without ceasing to be a man. Civil disobedience is never followed by anarchy. Criminal disobedience can lead to it. Every state puts down criminal disobedience by force. It perishes, if it does not. But to put down civil disobedience is to attempt to imprison consciousness." (Gandhi. Essential Writings 1991)

The world thus acquired a new method of combating injustice without violence and war. Gandhi and his family later returned to India, where they found a host of new injustices to the native people imposed by British rule. Gandhi joined the Indian National Congress Party, using again the tactics of non cooperation and passive resistance to obtain his ends, which finally resulted in India's obtaining Independence from Great Britain in 1947. This process involved great personal privations in that on many occasions Gandhi undertook personal fasting even to the point of threatened death in order to help his fellow countrymen.

The Universality of God

Gandhi showed the utmost humility and devotion in all of his activities which he attributed to God within him. He felt that God was universal through the world's great religions. He would read from the texts of the major faiths namely from Hinduism the Gita, from Christianity the Bible and from Islam the Koran. At first he equated God with Truth but later came to say that Truth was God. He stated:

> To see the universal and all-pervading Spirit of Truth face to face one must be able to love the meanest creation as oneself and a man who aspires after that cannot afford to keep out of any field of life. That is why my devotion to Truth has drawn me into the field of politics; and I can say without the slightest hesitation, and yet in all humility, that those who say that religion has nothing to do with politics do not know what religion means. (Gandhi. Essential Writings 1991)

Nonviolence (Ahimsa) and Adherence to Truth (Satyagraha)

These were the principles of action, or non action to be precise, that Gandhi promulgated and was able to promote by his extraordinary influence in India. Everything he did was on the basis of self sacrifice and personal example. He spent long periods in prison. He took up the cause of those otherwise without hope such as the Untouchables whom he rechristened as the Harijans (the children of God). These unfortunate individuals were marginalized in society having no real caste and having to undertake the most demeaning of work without the privileges of being able to visit temples or use the village well. He was desperately concerned about conflict between Hindus and Muslims taking a personal role in trying to prevent warfare at considerable danger to himself. He had infinite patience which was often essential as in his dealings with the Muslim leader, Muhammad Jinnah, who was said to be a man "with a problem for every solution"!

The Simple Life: Non Attachment

Gandhi believed in simplicity and hard work. He believed that every man benefited from simple toil such as growing his own food and spinning wool. Everything that he advocated, he applied to his own family and his own way of life. He set up several ashrams; the most important of these was at the final site of Sevagram where he practiced his simple views on life with a host of devoted followers. Sevagram was in central India in a very obscure rural area with intolerable heat in the middle part of the day. Despite its obscure position prominent politicians would find their way there and the Indian postal service was forced to establish a post office and a telegraph office there. Gandhi wanted all Indians to relearn the age old craft of hand spinning. This would enable the people of several hundred thousand impoverished villages to regain self-employment, self-reliance and self-respect. They would be encouraged to wear a rough white homespun cloth called *khadi*. This had repercussions for Lancashire, England, which had taken the textile industry from India. It was typical of Gandhi that he visited Lancashire to explain the situation to the workers there and trusted that they would understand, as indeed they appeared to do. He practiced vegetarianism and was a fructivore, eating mainly fruits and honey. That was very important to one's mental well being, Gandhi felt. The fructose sugar, unfortunately, was probably the cause of his famous toothless smile.

Bhakti—The Love of the Avatar

Christianity regards itself as being the only religion where God walked the earth—in the form of Jesus Christ. Hinduism, however, had the concept of the God Vishnu walking the earth in as many as nine forms, the so called Avatars of God. The most well known and beloved of these were Krishna and Rama. Devotional love of an Avatar is known in Hinduism as *bhakti*. Gandhi professed bhakti for both Krishna and Christ, seeing their messages as very similar in many respects. He was particularly influenced by the voice of Krishna in the Gita (*The Bhagavad-Gita*: part of the immense Indian epic the Mahabharata). In the Gita Krishna pronounces the famous passage:

> He is forever free who has broken
> out of the ego–cage of I and mine.
> To be united with the Lord of Love.
> This is the supreme state. Attain thou this
> and pass from death to immortality. (Bhaga-
> vad Gita. Parrinder Version)

Gandhi himself was regarded as a saint in India and many even regarded him as a god.

Repercussions of Gandhi's Example: The Life of Martin Luther King Jr.

Martin Luther King Jr., the black American leader, was much influenced by Gandhi's concept of non violent struggle. He was a Baptist minister who was a powerful leader of American Negros in their campaign for civil rights. He was always an opponent of violence and was awarded the Nobel Peace Prize in 1964. He was assassinated in Memphis Tennessee in 1968. It is ironic that Gandhi also died from an assassin's bullet, this time in 1948 at the hands of a fanatical Hindu who was incensed by Gandhi's efforts to achieve peace with the Muslim factions. If only Gandhi's methods of Ahimsa and Satyagraha could be applied to the current terrible situation in the Middle East the world would be in a very different situation. His example and his life's work are all too easily forgotten.

Other Examples of Multifaith Activity in the World

In the West, it is conventional to have only one religion. In the East, this has not always been the case. One must be mindful of China before the Cultural Revolution when it was customary to have three religions at the same time namely:

- Mahayana Buddhism for one's deepest philosophy
- Confucianism to tell one how to get on with one's fellow men and the importance of humanity.
- Taoism to acquaint one with the rhythms of nature and how to accommodate to them.

A similar triple faith pattern has been followed in Japan where another nature faith namely Shinto took the place of Taoism.

Brother Wayne Teasdale

It may seem a little paradoxical to pair up Gandhi, a major world figure, with Wayne Teasdale who tends only to be known in Spirituality circles. Gandhi is known to virtually everyone throughout the world whereas Wayne Teasdale is not a household name—for instance, he does not merit a mention in Wikipedia, the Google register of Notables! The two men came from totally different traditions and countries in that Gandhi was Indian brought up in the Hindu tradition while Teasdale was American with a Catholic background. However, both men had a similar vision of life and a similar inner heart.

Wayne Teasdale was born in 1945; his life only spanned fifty-nine years and yet in that time he underwent a remarkable spiritual development and achieved a great deal. He received his MA in philosophy from St. Joseph College and his PhD. in theology from Fordham University. He latterly became adjunct professor at DePaul University, Columbia College and the Catholic

Theological Union. In the latter part of his life he lived in the Catholic Theological Union in Chicago as a lay monk.

Teasdale was brought up in a Catholic family in Connecticut and his early ambition was to be a priest. However his faith was seriously shaken by the unrest of the sixties and the terrors of the Vietnam War. He became unsure about the immediacy and goodness of God being thrown into what he described as a three-year-long "dark night of the soul." A turning point in his life was when he enrolled in a retreat for laypeople run by Father Thomas Keating, the abbot of a monastery in Spencer, Massachusetts. Keating was highly revered as a mystic and advocate for inter faith dialogue between the world's religions. He opened Teasdale's mind to these two topics which were to become central to his whole future life. Subsequently, he came into correspondence with Father Beade Griffiths, a Benedictine monk who had settled in southern India with the intent to create a blend of Hinduism and Christianity. He was well known as a writer on this subject. Teasdale was to come to spend two years at Griffith's ashram, which opened his eyes to the whole field of Eastern mysticism. He undertook a set of renunciate vows under Griffiths, devoting himself to a life of simplicity, service and inter-spiritual search within the monastic tradition.

He came to serve on the board for the Parliament of the World's Religions and organized the bringing together of 8,000 people of different faiths for the 1993 Chicago Parliament. This led to 200 spiritual leaders signing "Guidelines for a Global Ethic." He was also behind the Synthesis Dialogues, moderated by the Dalai Lama, which was a forum bringing together key figures from a variety of professions and world faiths to examine the value and implications of mystical experience. He helped the Dalai Lama to draw up the far reaching and influential "Universal Declaration on Nonviolence."

The Mystic Heart

In the last three years of his short life, Teasdale wrote two books summarizing in a moving and evocative style his conclusions on mysticism and Interfaith dialogue during his years of monastic contemplation. They are:

- *The Mystic Heart*, 2001.
- *A Monk in the World: Cultivating a Spiritual Life*, 2003, combining with Ken Wilber, the influential transpersonal psychologist.

The Mystic Heart has a foreword written by the Dalai Lama, including this passage:

My good friend Brother Wayne Teasdale has long been actively involved in the effort to bring our religious traditions together. In this book Brother Wayne explores what he calls inter-spirituality. He shares his deep respect for and knowledge of the world's religions, relates examples from the lives of many great spiritual practitioners, and illuminates the traditions with great commonalities. *The Mystic Heart* is a work of great inspiration. (Teasdale 1999)

Teasdale explains his concept of the mystic heart as lying in the power, depths and ultimacy of mysticism and beauty where the human family's unity manifests itself. Liberation is expressed in the longing for the divine:

Every person is a mystic. The call to the spiritual journey is always inviting us. We need only respond. In this summons, in the cave of the heart, we are one.

A universal spirituality also has a place for various approaches to transformation from self-interest to other centered-ness, love, compassion, mercy and kindness. This labor of transformation is the work of the contemplative in all of us, and generously accepting that work permits us to cultivate our own mystic character. The mystic character grows out of humility of heart and simplicity of spirit, a radical openness to the real. The mystic heart is able to abandon the full self, the egoic life of the diluted self. (Teasdale 1999)

Teasdale forcibly points out that all of the world's religions have special insights and inspirations which can be combined. He states that inter spirituality, and the inter mystical life it entails, recognizes the larger community of human kind in the mystical quest. "It will realize that we all have a much greater heritage than simply our own tradition." (Teasdale 1999)

Furthermore, it acknowledges the validity of all genuinely spiritual experience. Inter-spirituality honors the totality of human spirituality insight, whether or not it is God-centered. To leave out spiritual experience is to impoverish humanity. Everything must be included, that is, everything that is authentic and genuine, that springs from contact with the divine, however we know or conceive of this.

In his final chapter entitled "Opening the Heart of the World" Teasdale outlines his vision in the search for a universal communal spirituality which is:

- It will be contemplative
- It will be interspiritual and intermystical
- It will be socially engaged
- It will be environmentally responsible

- It will be holistic
- It will engage other media in all of the arts, music and movies.
- It will be cosmically open.

In this inspiring path, Teasdale emphasizes that we must draw on our heritage and legacy of all man's total history of endeavor from his primitive roots to the present day. We may be free to combine world faiths, like the Jew who takes on a module of Buddhism (Bu-Jew), the Jew who has a regard for Christ (Christa-Jew), the Hindu with Buddhist leanings (Hindu-Bu) and so on. Judaism has suffered, and Buddhism takes on suffering more directly than any other faith; so it is logical to combine them. In fact, this linkage is sanctioned in Israel. Gandhi would definitely have approved.

THE LINKS BETWEEN GANDHI AND TEASDALE

Although these two men were from totally different traditions and geographic areas, with different temperaments, they both shared the mystic heart and a conviction that men and women can share faiths together. It is understandable that Teasdale mentions Gandhi in his book on three occasions. He felt that Gandhi's work was a permanent monument to the power and depth of nonviolence to change politics and society, to transform conflict into peaceful opportunities and to resolve differences. He cites Gandhi's life as an example of a life embracing quality and simplicity. "The Sanyasin has only two pieces of cloth (a dhoti and a shawl for his clothing), a walking stick, and begging bowl. Mahatma Gandhi himself lived in this manner. He was completely committed to simplicity of life and lifestyle; he lived disposed of the goods of this earth." (Teasdale 1999)

He explains that Gandhi knew how distracting those goods could be, how they become sources of division and conflict. He mentions Gandhi in relationship to the economic sphere where he was very clear on this point. He eloquently applied the truth of simplicity of lifestyle. The earth has enough for mankind's needs but not for its greeds! Simplicity is at once an inner lure of the spiritual life and a basic demand of justice and wise economics: "It has perhaps taken the ecological crisis to prove that Mahatma was right." (Teasdale 1999)

Answer: Certainly, it is possible to combine
religions with great effect as shown by these two saintly
men, and as in the triple way of erstwhile China.

Reading List and Sources

Gandhi the Man. Eknath Easwaran. Nilgiri Press. Second Edition 1983.

The Mystic Heart. Discovering a Universal Spirituality in the World's Religions. Wayne Teasdale. New World Library. 2001.

CHAPTER 12. TRANS FAITH: FRED HOYLE AND PAUL DAVIES

Question: Is it possible to start to use all of the rich foundation of human philosophic and religious thought as a basis for a totally cosmic new viewpoint on our life and faith on this miraculous planet of ours?

Thinking Outside the Box!

We have looked at a variety of worldviews as an aid to discerning meaning, namely:

- Existentialism and Post Modernism.
- The Philosopher's Viewpoint.
- Atheism.
- Sensualism.
- Mysticism.
- Agnosticism.
- The Primatologist's Viewpoint.
- The Neuroscientist's Viewpoint.
- Unifaith.
- Interfaith.
- Multifaith.

These are a variety of ways of looking at "this strange eventful history" which is our life. All of these viewpoints, in one way or another, involve a consideration of religion it its widest sense. The particular viewpoint may deny religion or incorporate religion in a single source or multi-source derivation. As human beings, a decision about religion seems to be vitally important to us either in its acceptance or in its denial. It will make a great deal of difference to the kind of meaning that we derive from life. Even the view of the Existentialist, allows us to make the choice between being a religious person or a non-religious person, even though existence is seen as essentially meaningless. If we are honest with ourselves, we may have to come to the conclusion that all of the Theistic Religions are based on quasi magical, semi-mythical precepts. Is it possible, to develop a new viewpoint which eliminates magic and myth as far as possible but still allows a religious viewpoint in that we experience life with awe and gratitude as a path towards ultimate meaning. We are about to examine a man who provides one such viewpoint, and that is Fred Hoyle.

A SCIENTIFIC VISIONARY: SIR FRED HOYLE

He lived a long and extraordinarily productive life from the viewpoint of his writings and activities from 1915 to 2001. Here is the first paragraph from his affectionate obituary written by his pupil and colleague Martin Rees, who was Astronomer Royal at that time in the United Kingdom:

> Fred Hoyle's varied and prolific outlook spanned more than 60 years. Indeed, throughout the entire period 1945–1970 he was preeminent among astrophysicists in the range and influence of his contributions. His engaging wit and relish for controversy, which he retained throughout his long life, gained him a high public profile. He had a wide following as a popularizer of science and as a successful writer of science fiction. He also played an active organizational role in science. Hoyle died on August 20, 2001 in Bournemouth, England. (Rees 2001)

Giving his lectures, Sir Hoyle was not impressive at first glance, being a shortish Yorkshire man. But his deep sincerity, sense of humor and profound intelligence soon gave his audiences the strong conviction of being in the presence of a genius with a refreshingly new way of viewing human life on this planet and a wider viewpoint of existence in the cosmos, of which he had a special awareness in view of his role as an astro-physicist. Hoyle was such a genius and he can help to bring us to a refreshingly new paradigm for the 21st century and beyond.

Hoyle's Life

A genius or revolutionary figure may arise frequently from an apparently obscure background and this is so with Hoyle. He was born on June 24, 1915, in Bingley, Yorkshire. His parents were a wool merchant and a teacher. There was no privilege in his upbringing; he attended the local grammar school—but so, reputedly, did Shakespeare! From this mundane background, he quickly started to demonstrate his great talents by gaining a scholarship to the prestigious Cambridge University, where at Emmanuel College he first studied mathematics. The boy from Yorkshire quickly found his feet in that elitist environment by winning the Cambridge Mayhew Prize for his outstanding performance. He later shifted towards astro-physics under the stimulation of Raymond Lyttleton, although always applying a mathematical viewpoint in his subsequent work.

The Nature of Hoyle's New Vision

In his early life, Hoyle was a pragmatist and a declared atheist. He later changed his stance towards life in very significant ways. He was always pragmatic but came to combine that with a sense of great wonder at life's extraordinary complexity and at the features of the universe that allowed our existence. His atheism changed to a conviction that there was Intelligence at work in the Cosmos although its nature might be very different from the anthropomorphic images of conventional theistic religion. He was never hampered by the reductionist viewpoint which characterized so much of 20th century science. He was not afraid to use a teleological approach seeking meaning within the phenomena which he examined. The breadth of his intellect enabled him to make new formulations on the most fundamental questions particularly:

- Our Atomic Origin from the Stars.
- The Origins of the Universe.
- A Cosmic Origin for Life: Panspermia.
- The Origin of Species Apart from Darwinism.
- A Concept of Intelligent Design.

Let us examine each of these viewpoints because they can be the basis for a new way of looking at our existence and allow us to see that existence in a religious way unhampered by magic and myth.

Hoyle believed that it was the duty of the Scientist to be at the forefront of progress. Plato had the viewpoint that a community leader should be a

Philosopher as expounded in the Republic. In all truth, Hoyle was both Scientist and Philosopher. Let us outline each of these contributions.

Our Atomic Origin from the Stars

It has been stated that there is little doubt that Hoyle's most lasting and significant contribution to science concerns the origin of the elements of life. His theory of nuclear genesis (the build-up of the elements in the hot interiors of stars) was felt to be an outstanding scientific landmark of the 1950's. He worked with the Institute of Technology in Pasadena and with Jeffery and Margaret Burbridge. It is recorded that, in the development of this theory, Hoyle also collaborated with W.A. Fowler of the California Institute. Here is a quote from another obituary, this time by the distinguished astronomer Bernard Lovell:

> Hither to, the general belief was that all the elements must have been produced in the hot primordial universe. Hoyle's paper, on the contrary, showed that the elements could be produced from the primordial hydrogen by nuclear-synthesis in the hot interior of stars. The theory gave a satisfactory account of the relative abundances of the elements, provided an explanation of the direction of stellar evolution and gave an objective basis for calculation of the internal constitution of stars.

> The theory also confirmed a prediction of Hoyle's that there must be an excited state of the carbon 12 isotope—at the energy he had predicted from a consideration of the evolution of red giant stars. This incidentally, was agreeably consistent with the steady state cosmological theory, since there was no necessity for an initial hot condition of a primordial universe. (Lovell, 2001)

Fowler was awarded the Nobel Prize for physics in 1983 mainly for this work undertaken with Hoyle and it is felt by many that Hoyle should have been included in the award. However it is rumored in the scientific community that the Royal Swedish Academy may have been wary of giving a Nobel Prize to someone who was felt to possibly suffer from a form of scientific madness, in view of his revolutionary views of such subjects as Panspermia, to be discussed shortly. Many geniuses have been treated in similar ways by their colleagues who lack such novel vision.

The Origin of the Universe: A Steady State Multibang Alternative

The current majority view of the scientific community is that the universe was created in a single cataclysmic event from nothing. This extraordinary event may well strain the credulity of the ordinary man but it particularly strained the belief of Hoyle. He was the first person to describe that theory by the term "Big Bang"—he did this in a radio talk, in a somewhat derisory manner. The term has stuck and is now used throughout the world. Hoyle propounded with colleagues Hermann Bondi and Thomas Gold an alternative continuous creation theory which acquired the name of the steady state theory. I will quote Bernard Lovell once again:

> Hoyle's theory had stressed the philosophical aspect of a perfect cosmological principle in which the universe would have a higher degree of uniformity not only in space but also in time, therefore evading the scientific problem associated with a beginning and a finite passed time. Hoyle dealt with continuous creation of the primordial hydrogen that would be essential to maintain the steady state, and placed the concept within the framework of general relativity. (Lovell, 2001)

Until the discovery of the cosmic microwave background in 1965, the observational evidence was inconclusive between the two theories but the cosmic microwave evidence tended to support the "big bang" universe. Hoyle was unconvinced and continued to justify his concept that the universe was eternal although he conceded that there may have been various big bangs in its history. It was typical of the man, that he was able in the last year before his life to be the principal editor of a book entitled *A Different Approach to Cosmology*, in which he produced the detailed scientific and mathematical basis of his judgment. This can be termed The Steady State Multi Bang Theory. In fact, the universe oscillated between expansion and contraction. Time will tell who is correct. If I were a betting man and had the financial means to support it, I would put big money on Hoyle.

The Cosmic Origin of Life: Panspermia

Hoyle could not accept the current reductionist scientific viewpoint that life itself had been created by random processes over vast periods of time. He wrote:

> The entire structure of orthodox biology still holds that life arose at random. Yet as biochemists discover more and more about the awesome complexity of life, it is apparent that the chances of it originating by accident are so minute that they can be completely ruled out Life cannot have arisen by chance. (Hoyle, 1983)

Hoyle calculated that the chances of the random creation of a single enzyme (the worker molecules in the cells which are catalysts) would be fifty trillion trillion to one against. He points out that there are at least two thousand different enzymes in every cell emphasizing the virtual impossibility of life having started by non directed means. He expounded this view with scientific data in his book *Mathematics of Evolution*, published in 1999. Hoyle famously stated that the odds of life occurring accidentally were similar to the odds of a gale blowing through a scrap yard and assembling a Boeing 757. He had the ability to bring things home to people using his blunt North Country wit.

Darwin had commented in a letter that life probably commenced in "some small warm pond on earth." Hoyle's vision was much wider—he felt that life had been created elsewhere in the cosmos. It had arrived on earth in the form of virus-like and bacterial particles which probably permeate space and account for the spectrographic qualities of interstellar dust. How did these living seeds reach the earth? Most probably in the tails of comets. This was the theory of Panspermia promulgated in the early years of the century by the Swedish scientist Arrhenius. One must be mindful of the fact that Francis Crick, joint discoverer of the structure of DNA, was also certain that life could not have originated on this planet, surmising that it may have arrived via a space ship. I prefer Hoyle's theory! Hoyle clothed the theory with scientific data and his overall view of the cardinal role of the cosmos in life.

He published a second seminal book in the last year of his life, entitled *Astronomical Origins of Life. Steps Towards Panspermia*. Here he collaborated with his previous student and latterly colleague Professor N.C. Wickramasinghe. Hoyle enlarges the canvas of our existence in a way which can change our view of ourselves in a revolutionary way.

The Origin of Species Apart From Darwin

Darwin saw his concept of natural selection as the explanation for the evolution of all species found on earth. The change from one species to another occurred by the spontaneous occurrence of small changes or mutations. If a mutation was favorable to survival then it would be incorporated into the creature's genetic background and could, via a process of small increments, lead to the production of a totally new species. Hoyle regarded this as a simplistic inadequate theory as expressed here: "Is natural selection really the powerful idea it is popularly supposed to be? As long ago as my teens, I found it puzzling that so many people seem to think so, because the more I thought about it, the more circular the argument seemed to become." (Hoyle 1983)

The circular argument could be stated thus: "If among a number of varieties of a species one is best fitted to survive in the environment as it happens to be, then it is the variety that is best fitted to survive that will best survive." Surely, Hoyle argued the rich assembly of plants and animals found on Earth cannot have been produced by a truism of this minor order? He suggested that the spark of evolution must lie elsewhere: it lies in the source of the variations by which natural selection operates. He pointed out that Darwinians believe nowadays that the ultimate source lies in chance miscopyings of genetic information, a view which he believed to be quite erroneous.

There is now a growing reassessment of Darwinism. It is obvious that Darwin changed the way that the Victorian world viewed itself so that it had to acknowledge a link with the other species on this earth not regarding itself as totally unique and superior. The record of the rocks in the form of fossils, however, does not adequately show a regular series of transitional forms. There is no doubt that natural selection explains microevolution. If you happen to be a fox, in an arctic region, your survival will be favored by the color of your fur—if it is lighter than the other foxes then this will help your particular variant to be the predominant one in that particular background. This had been termed by Herbert Spencer "survival of the fittest." It does not however give an adequate explanation for the macro-evolution of new species rather than variations. The theory of punctuated evolution suggested by Gould and Etheridge is a better description whereby new species appear to arrive suddenly and in a punctuated manor. There is still the need to provide an explanation for the mechanism. There appears to be a genetic clock ticking—the occurrence of new species being metaphorically like the striking of the hours. Hoyle as well as mathematically refuting Darwinian evolution, added his own concept for the explanation.

Hoyle called upon the concept of Panspermia for a theory of cosmic gene injection. Virus like particles coming in from outer space could invade the human genome and either dramatically or insidiously alter its evolution even to the point of producing a new species. At first sight, this seems a mind boggling suggestion but one is conversant with the fact that viruses are known, in medicine, to gain ingress into a cell producing so called oncogenes which cause the cell to transform into a malignant or cancer variant. Hoyle foresaw this aspect as in the following quotation:

Do we need proof that viruses and other microorganisms are being added to the Earth from outside? The problem in seeking an answer to this question is to distinguish between new microorganisms coming in from outside from the ones that are here already. However if some among the new organisms are able to cause disease in terrestrial plants and animals there is a chance that the new and the old can be distinguished. (Hoyle, 1983)

Hoyle even speculated during lectures that influenza epidemics might be caused by the ingress of viruses from outer space. This was one of the theories that led to Hoyle being regarded as eccentric in his viewpoint. He has produced much evidence as exhibited in the book *Diseases From Space*, published in 1979 with C. Wickramasinghe. Again, time will test the truth of this concept. In the field of paleontology, there is great speculation as to why so many of the major groups of organisms appeared suddenly in what is known as the Cambrian Explosion at around 550 million years ago. Hoyle felt that this could have been due to injection of genetic material from outer space even in the form of small creatures, rather than micro-organisms, incorporated in dormant states in meteorites and other forms of intergalactic projectiles.

A Concept of Intelligent Design

As a result of the work presented, Hoyle started to change his atheistic views to consider the operation of Intelligence outside the Earth. Hoyle posed several questions:
- Where is this intelligence located?
- Exactly what does it do?
- What is its physical form?

In his seminal book "The Intelligent Universe" he states that a generation or more of scientific consolidation is needed before risking an answer for such ambitious questions. Attempts to answer them are otherwise only too likely to become engulfed in a vague, inaccurate wave of scientific fiction, he states. Nevertheless, there was a more restricted question of this kind he had been asking himself as he walked the hills and valleys around his home in the English Lake District: "Is intelligence outside the Earth inaccessibly remote, or is it close enough to be contacted if only we knew how?" (Hoyle, 1983)

Hoyle considered what the nature of such an intelligence might be. He pointed out that there is a definite limit to the capacity of an intelligence, such as that of a human being, in an embodied form. In a planet such as our own with gravity, the head housing the central nervous system has a limit to its size in that the subject has to support it against gravity and also it must be capable of being delivered through a human pelvis. Therefore an unlimited intelligence might be in some other form altogether. He made the somewhat startling suggestion that is could even be gaseous! Then there would then be no limit to its capacity. Hoyle fancifully explored this concept in his popular novel *The Black Cloud* published in 1957. A cloud of gas, of which there are a vast number in the universe, approaches the solar system on a course which is predicted to bring it between the Sun and the Earth, shutting off the sun's rays. The cloud demonstrated a profound intelligence and was able to communicate with a startled scientific and political community before moving off into outer space.

Where could such intelligence be located in the universe—either in gaseous or other form? One is mindful of the concept of "dark matter" which, in some estimates, is felt to occupy ninety five percent of all matter. It is said to account for a problem in the gravitational environment across the universe: clusters of matter, such as gas clouds or groups of galaxies, appear to behave as though the gravitational field they inhabited was stronger than could be accounted for by the matter that could be observed in the vicinity. It has been proposed that this extra gravitational force could originate from some "dark" invisible matter. There is another complimentary concept of "dark energy" which is thought to be responsible for the increasing dispersion of the galaxies.

Hoyle's concept of an intelligent universe can be seen as the precursor of the current school of Intelligent Design. Indeed Hoyle did see intelligence to be at work in the creation of life rather than the blind force of Darwinism. This concept was taken up by the biochemist and medical doctor Michael Denton, the biochemist Michael Behe, the mathematician and theologian William Dembski, and the analytic lawyer Philip Johnson although the movement seems all too easily, to forget its debt to Hoyle. It can also be easily confused with fundamentalist biblical creationism as has occurred in recent court cases initiated to prevent school children being taught this concept as by the use of the children's textbook *Of Pandas and People*, by Charles Phaxton. It was felt that this contravened federal regulations about teaching specific religious data in schools although Hoyle would have been appalled at such an interpretation.

Hoyle's Use of Fiction to Express Concepts as Yet Unproven

Hoyle was a great communicator with an ability to express his ideas at many different levels such as to the scientific world, the man in the street, and even children. He was a successful novelist as mentioned in the case of *The Black Cloud*. He saw the novel as a way of letting his imagination and fantasy roam in a very creative manner. He could express intuitive ideas which would have no place in an objective scientific context. He was often joined by his son John Elliot Hoyle, as a co-author—Hoyle would provide the scientific idea and his son would create characters to clothe the plot. For example, the two of them co-wrote the BBC television serials "A For Andromeda" (1961) and "Andromeda Breakthrough" (1962). In Hoyle's novels, the heroes are scientists, who are opposed by politicians—a situation which Hoyle experienced very often in his own life. Alien or cosmic intelligence is often beyond human comprehension, but also can be dangerously ignorant of the value of human kind making the stuff of drama. Hoyle, in his fiction, was intrigued by the problems of communication with an outside intelligence as in his statement: "But I had an intelligent life form in the story that didn't think in words, a form that had to learn words before it could communicate with man. This was an integral part of the plot of the Cloud. It was only after the scientist learned to communicate that the cloud was persuaded to leave the solar system, on the way encouraging human kind to create more geniuses." (Hoyle, 1957)

Summing up Hoyle's Contribution

Fred Hoyle just lived into the 21st century, reaching his 86th birthday on June 24, 2001. Six weeks later he had the last of a series of strokes and died on August 20. His longtime colleague, Jeffery Burbidge from the Center For Astrophysics and Space Sciences in the University of California at San Diego, summed up Hoyle's contribution in an after dinner speech on the day of celebration for Fred Hoyle's life and his science in Cambridge on the 16th of April 2002:

> In sixty years of research, Fred had a huge number of ideas. Like all very great scientists he was not afraid to be wrong. In my view, he was much more often right than wrong, because he was always guided by the evidence (all of it, and by an excellent intuition). In the latter part of his career his view diverged a long way from what most people want to believe, particularly in cosmology and high-energy astrophysics. Much of the difficulty here, in my view, has been due to the fact that ideas about origins and cosmology, in general,

are being driven more today by sociology than by scientific evidence. Eventually we (or some of us) will know the answer. As a betting man, I will wager that again, in this second round of the battle between Galileo and the Vatican, Galileo (in the person of Fred) will win. Finally let us drink a toast to a great man whose achievements have lifted us all: to Fred Hoyle. (Burbridge, 2002)

We might liken Fred Hoyle to Galileo in order to sum up the pattern of resistance that he met from certain quarters in the world of astronomy. It led to his resigning his Plumian Professorship at the University of Cambridge at the early age of 57. He sums up his attitude as follows: "I do not see any sense in continuing to skirmish on a battle field where I can never hope to win. The Cambridge system is effectively designed to prevent one ever establishing a directed policy—key decisions can be upset by ill-informed and politically motivated committees. To be effective in this system one must forever be watching one's colleagues, almost like a Robespierre spy system. If one does so, then of course little time is left for any real science." (Hoyle, Letter 2001)

Hoyle's autobiography is entitled appropriately *Home Is Where the Wind Blows.* He was always something of an outsider. He did have the recognition of being elected to Fellowship of the Royal Society (the top accolade for a scientist in the UK) and conferment of a knighthood—Sir Fred Hoyle. Fortunately Hoyle had a soul mate in his wife Barbara who understood his work and supported him in all things. When leaving Cambridge, they sought solace in nature, going to live in a remote farmhouse on Cockley Moor near Ullswater, in the Lake District of Northwest England. Barbara undertook the task of transforming the overgrown gardens. Hoyle was able to go for long walks in the hills to return to play his classical music recordings—he found deep solace in Beethoven. Hoyle found great inspiration in nature and particularly hill walking.

After his retirement from Cambridge, Hoyle began a hugely productive collaboration with his former pupil Chandra Wickramasinghe who had been appointed Professor of Applied Mathematics and Astronomy at Cardiff University in Wales. Together they wrote over 200 articles in professional journals. They summed up their common attitude as follows:

The ideas we have described both singly and taken together, represent radical departures from currently accepted beliefs in science. Scientists as a rule are reluctant to accept such change, but as we have indicated, the changes of Dogma are dictated, almost invariably by the facts that have emerged. Through our long history as a thinking species we have always been loath to accept the theory of the world in which we ourselves did not occupy a central and most important place. The view that the Earth was the center of the solar system was held for centuries, and was abandoned only with great anguish after Copernicus. We have now come to accept the position that the solar system itself is not the center of the galaxy, and that our galaxy itself is not the center of the Universe. Likewise, the same Copernican—style revolution must be applied to life. Life, with its extraordinary subtlety of design and its exceedingly intricate complexity, could only have evolved on a scale that transcends the scale of our planet, the size of the solar system, even perhaps the size of the entire galaxy. (Gregory, 2005)

Hoyle and Buddhism

Hoyle suggested putting aside the older beliefs until some rational basis for discussing them has been achieved. This seemed to apply to the theistic religions as he clearly had a high regard for Buddhism, as evidenced by this quotation from the final page of the book *Our Place in the Cosmos*, written with his co-worker Professor Chandra Wickramsinghe:

> Gautama Buddha stressed....on his death bed...take refuge only in truth. This is exemplary advice to a young scientist, even in the present day. Buddha's own vision of the world was also remarkably post-Copernican, even in the 6th century BC. He describes a Universe composed of billions of "Minor World Systems," each of which resembles our own planetary system...Throughout the dialogues it is abundantly clear that Buddha viewed life and consciousness (which he thought to be associated with all life) as cosmic phenomena, linked inextricably with the structure of the Universe as a whole." (Hoyle and Wickramsinghe, 1993)

He commented that if such traditions eventually prevail, science may at last come to be freed of its medieval fetters.

PAUL DAVIES: A ONETIME STUDENT OF HOYLE

Paul Davies is an internationally acclaimed physicist and cosmologist who is currently a professor at Arizona State University where he is the director of Beyond, a research institute dedicated to the study of fundamental concepts in science. Like Hoyle, he has a great ability to communicate complex scientific concepts, particularly related to the cosmos, and is the author of twenty seven books on topics ranging from black holes to life on Mars. He is however far from being just a popularizer of science and has to his credit two hundred research papers. Like Hoyle, one of his main preoccupations has been to study the concept of Intelligence behind life and one of his best known books is *The Mind of God, Science and the Search for Ultimate Meaning*. Davies was a research fellow at the Institute of Theoretical Astronomy in Cambridge where Fred Hoyle was the director and Brandon Carter a fellow researcher. Carter was later to propound the so called "Anthropic Principle" which detailed how the universe appeared to be fine tuned to allow the emergence of carbon based life. This was in the late 1960s and it proved to be a very influential factor in Davies's thinking. Most of Davies's books have a number of references to Fred Hoyle. Before going to Cambridge, Davies had obtained a doctorate in physics from University College, London. Like Hoyle, he is British-born. He obviously has a restless nature that enjoys new challenges for he has held a variety of academic appointments in the University of Newcastle upon Tyne, the University of Adelaide in Australia and Macquarie University. His profound interest in the possibility of the presence of intelligent life elsewhere in the cosmos is exemplified by the fact that in 2005 he took up the Chair of SETI (Search for Extraterrestrial Intelligence) in the Post-Detection Science and Technology Task Group of the International Academy of Astronautics. Richard Dawkins mentions Davies in his book *The God Delusion* as one of a group of physicists who occasionally slip into the language of religious metaphor, as follows:

> Paul Davies's *The Mind of God* seems to hover somewhere between Einsteinian pantheism and an obscure form if deism—for which he was rewarded with the Templeton Prize (a very large sum of money given annually by the Templeton foundation usually to a scientist who is prepared to say something nice about religion). (Dawkins 2006)

He therefore got off fairly lightly from Dawkin's scathing tongue! An anonymous reviewer of *The Mind of God* comments, "His ideas seem a strange mixture of Cartesian reductionism on the one hand and mystical idealism on the other." Like Hoyle, he is always provocative and contentious.

The Influence of Fred Hoyle on Paul Davies

One of Davies's recent books is titled *The Fifth Miracle: The Search for the Origin and Meaning of Life*. He explains that he took the title from the mythical five miracles recounted in the book of Genesis, describing how God made the world:

- creation of the universe

- creation of light
- creation of the firmament
- the creation of dry land
- the creation of vegetation

He quotes Genesis 1:11, "let the land produce vegetation." There are a number of references in this book to Hoyle's influence. He states that he could trace his interest in these matters (the origin of life or biogenesis) back to his days as a student of physics at University College, London in the 1960s. Like many of his friends, he read Fred Hoyle's famous science-fiction novel *The Black Cloud*, about the arrival in the solar system of a large cloud of gas from an interstellar space. Such clouds were well known to astronomers but Hoyle's intriguing idea was to suppose that they could be alive.

> Now, this was a poser. How can a cloud be alive? I puzzled over it at length. Surely gas clouds just obey the laws of physics? How could they exhibit autonomous behavior, have thoughts, make choices? But, then, it occurred to me, all living organisms supposedly obey the laws of physics. Hoyle's brilliance was in using the example of a cloud to draw out that paradox in a stark manner. (Davies 1999)

He records that *The Black Cloud* left him baffled and vaguely disturbed. What exactly, he wondered, is life? And how did it get started? Might there be something funny going on inside living organisms? These ideas circulated in his mind, he records, over the next decade and by this time he relates that he found himself again influenced by the ideas of Hoyle and also those of Dyson and Gold. Dyson, he recalled, speculated on the origin of life, letting his imagination run free over the future and ultimate fate of technological civilizations. Gold had a theory that large quantities of hydrocarbons lay trapped under the ground: when a search was made to test his hypothesis, new subterranean life forms were discovered. All these developments helped shape his thinking on the subject, particularly Hoyle's original thinking on the origin of life: "Hoyle, with collaborator Chandra Wickramasinghe, daringly suggested that maybe life did not originate on earth at all, but was brought here by comets" (Davies, 1999).

In the book Davies devotes a whole chapter to Panspermia, a topic which many scientists reject out of hand. He examines the subject at length, with respect, and acknowledges that Hoyle's work brought this notion to his attention. He knew that for the past twenty years, Fred Hoyle and Chandra Wickramasinghe, in the face of much skepticism, had been pushing the theory that comets contain living organisms. They offered support for their idea through an analysis of medical records, and claimed that the passage of comets into the earth's atmosphere correlated with the outbreak of diseases. They suggested that various pandemics, such as the great Justinian Plague of AD 540, in which possibly one hundred million people died, were actually of extraterrestrial origin.

Hoyle and Wickramasinghe did not suppose that life in space is restricted to comets. They backed Arrhenius's original proposal that individual microbes can float unprotected around the galaxy: "Pointing to the fact that many interstellar grains are about the size of bacteria, they argue that substantial quantities of material in interstellar space are actually of biological origin. As evidence for this audacious theory, they cite the fact that the infrared spectrum of dry E. coli looks uncannily close to that of interstellar dust" (Davies 1999).

Davies does however point out that the panspermia theory evades the question of the ultimate site of biogenesis. He examines whether this could have been on Mars, as one site which may have had life at one time and seeded the Earth. In commenting about this underlying problem of biogenesis, he makes his celebrated statement "life seems just to good to be true." He also examines Hoyle's Steady State Theory and comments, "there is no known fundamental reason why the universe cannot have always existed." He reasoned that because a steady-state universe has infinite age, it was possible to imagine that life might also have existed forever. Then neither cosmos nor life would have had an origin. As long as there is a way for organisms to get from old galaxies to new ones, life need never have formed de novo from inert chemicals. The problem of biogenesis was therefore completely sidestepped. It was not necessary to adhere to the steady-state cosmology as such to avoid an origin of life. "Provided that the Universe is infinitely old and has some sort of replenishment process and as long as microbes can find a way to travel safely from one place to another, then life may always have been a property of the universe" (Davies, 1999).

He pointed out that this is precisely what Hoyle and Wickramasinghe had proposed! Davies does however acknowledge the merits of the rival Big Bang theory. He has a tendency to be ambivalent on a number of occasions as though he does not want to back a theory too strongly for fear of being wrong—who can blame him! In his most recent book, *Cosmic Jackpot: Why Our Universe is Just Right for Life*, Davies examines at length the concept of intelligent design and Darwinism. He states: "It is obvious that chance alone would be no more likely to produce a living cell than (to use Fred Hoyle's famous analogy) a whirlwind blowing through a junkyard would produce a Boeing 747. Chance was not alone in fashioning the biosphere" (Davies 2007).

He then goes into another slightly ambivalent phase and is concerned that Intelligent Design is a revival of the old God-of-the-gaps viewpoint. He also sees it as a revival of the design theory for God's existence and states: "Many features of the human body contain design flaws, such as the danger-ous convergence of food and air pathways in the throat and the inadequate robustness of the spine. If there is a designer, then this being is not micro-managing the process very well" (Davies, 2007).

There is no doubt that Davies was greatly influenced by Hoyle in his training in Cambridge and is forever reexamining Hoyle's philosophy, even though at times he is nervous about accepting all its far reaching implica-tions and wishes to examine the whole field of discussion, which is so rife at this moment.

> Answer: Both of these men, through their original thought, allow us to glimpse a new vision of Cosmic Intelligence, not confined to anthropomorphic form, and a concept of common life seeded throughout the universe— which brings entirely new depths of meaning into play.

Reading List and Sources
Fred Hoyle's Universe. Jane Gregory. Oxford University Press 2005.
The Intelligent Universe. Fred Hoyle. Michael Joseph, London 1983
The Fifth Miracle. Paul Davies. Simon & Schuster. 1999.

CHAPTER 13. THIS STRANGE EVENTFUL HISTORY

RICK WARREN AND DANIEL DENNET

Question: Can we find a Purpose Driven Life incorporating a new concept of Faith which is Cosmic in outlook and capable of generating true happiness in an environment of a General Organizing Design?

THE PATH WE HAVE FOLLOWED SO FAR

We have examined a series of pairs of individuals whose lives have been lived with great passion and sincerity, sometimes at their own hazard. Each of these pairs of lives has the potential to instruct us in rethinking our own life to find meaning in this Strange Eventful History so redolent with promise and hazard.

Let us examine some of the points that they illustrate:

Existentialism and Postmodernism (Sartre and Foucault):

Here we are starting with a blank canvas. This philosophy teaches that nothing has any ultimate meaning but we can choose to perceive a meaning like selecting a brush or color in painting. This exercise will help us to escape from our own inner Nausea. The bigger the brush and the bolder the color, the more positive may be our chosen image. We may well wish to distrust the authoritarianism of past ages and look afresh at life. In a way, we repeat the experience of Descartes with his seminal saying "I think, therefore I am"—we have a new basic starting point in a new age. Victor Frankl cautions against a too strict adherence to existential nihilism by reminding us of the importance of a goal or a special person in finding meaning—conclusions from the concentration camps.

The Philosophers (Socrates and the Buddha):

With both of these thinkers, we set out to derive with them a meaningful path working from first principles. Socrates chose the Dialectical Method while the Buddha selected the way of Meditation and Inner Reserves. Both were totally frank in their approach. Socrates sought the roots of Goodness and Eros. On the other hand, the Buddha confronted life's suffering and impermanence. He was able to describe a way to a far shore of inner calm and changelessness namely Nirvana.

The Atheists (Freud and Dawkins)

Both of these honest but uncompromising men have sought to define a life free of what they saw as the stultifying concept of an all powerful sometimes wrathful God. They certainly present us with a blank canvas although at first sight it may seem a canvas with a gaping hole in its center. We may detect a certain aridity and savageness in their attitude but it is important to appreciate the frankness of their position.

The Sensualists (Gauguin and Van Gogh):

The lives and work of these two men give us vibrant color and drama allowing us to experience one potent way of escaping the tyranny of Schopenhauer's terrifying Will. Both enabled us to see the visual world with new eyes and to explore the passions of their inner lives. The way of the Senses is a great gift but it may encroach too nearly on the ancient left hand path with all its hazards if we do not handle it carefully!

The Mystics (Jung and Eliade):

The Mystic seeks a direct union with the reality behind life. Jung's theory of the Archetypes allows us to recognize those timeworn and hallowed images in the context of a Collective Unconscious, whether inherited or painstakingly acquired. Mircea Eliade explored every religious system in a tireless search for meaning seeming to choose the sacredness of nature (or sacrality, as he called it) as an inspiration for the great variety of holy imagery. Truly Nature is a source of inspiration and challenge particularly if we take on Intelligent Design! Once we have grasped the concept of the Archetype and The Symbol we start to see everything in life in not just a specific context but in a general context that embellishes it.

The Agnostics and Doubters (Darwin and Behe):

Here are two thinkers confronting man's long process of evolution as a vital backdrop for our attempt to understand life. Both tried their utmost to see the Tree of Life in terms of theistic religion but each came to an agnostic or questioning position. This was more frank in the case of Darwin but shows through in Behe's latest statements although he certainly cannot discard a concept of God. However, he begins to wince at the consequences of that belief as conveyed literally in the statements of scripture and a survey of the savageness of many aspects of life.

The Primatologists (De Wall and King)

If we are in doubt of the true nature of man, it seems reasonable to explore the nature of his predecessors in the Chain of Being. For example, are we deep down more akin to the aggressive paternalistic chimpanzee or the easy going more maternalistic, sexy bonobo, or, as is more likely, a mixture of both? In the long trudging path of the hominids, can we discern the emergence of the roots of compassion early on in a certain "belongingness." Is this belongingness just an evolutionary survival mechanism or does it show an early blossoming of our most precious aspect, that of compassion, as an example of what may be built into Intelligent Design.

The Neuroscientists (MacLean and Persinger):

Can we face up to the implications of a suggested triple brain comprising the reptilian brain stem with its capacity for harsh aggression, the mammalian brain with the development of the limbic system with its capacity for emotion but also the herd instinct, and finally the primate human brain with its development of the cerebral cortex. In the latter lies the fourth brain of the pre-frontal lobes which enable us to use prior cognitive knowledge and the possibility to inhibit or say "no" to the reflex dictates of reptilian aggression and mammalian herd instinct. Is Persinger correct to postulate that we have a mystical religious center(s) in our cerebrum centered in the right temporo-parietal zone which enables us to have episodes of release in time and space with flashes of unitive linkage with the cosmos or the intrusion of a Sensed Presence of something or someone beyond? Alternatively is the religious brain more widely based than this in the central nervous system?

The Unifaith Stance (Teilhard De Chardin and Collins)

Here we meet two men, both eminent scientists, choosing to see life as the expression of a single faith system and seeking an Omega Point, to use Chardin's poignant term. We are all certainly part of a great thinking Noosphere, again to use Chardin's expression, but should we think ourselves into this exclusivity position. This viewpoint will work to give a life of great apparent inner meaning but can we offer it to all of our companions on this earth in other faith systems with the honesty of a Socrates or the Buddha?

Interfaith (Hick and the Dalai Lama)

Here, in the work of these two men, we can embrace a viewpoint that lets us hold out our arms to all our brothers in the world in an attitude of reverent awe and curiosity. Are there different faiths for the temperaments of different people, as the tolerant Dalai Lama suggests? We can do well to meditate on John Hick's Common Points of the World's Religions namely:

- A cosmic optimism that all will be well
- The centrality in the world's faiths of Compassion (Agape, Koruna, Selfless Love): the so called Golden Rule.
- The change that religion should produce in an individual is from Self Centeredness to Reality Centeredness.

In this viewpoint, we have the possibility to debate honestly and respectfully amongst ourselves the true nature of that Reality.

Multifaith (Gandhi and Teasdale)

Maybe we don't have to choose! Maybe we can have our cake and eat it by taking on aspects of multiple belief systems. One is mindful of the old Chinese Triple Way of:

- Buddhism for one's deepest philosophy.
- Confucianism to teach us of the special wonder and duties of being human.
- Taoism to instruct us in the rhythms of Nature and to persuade us to go with the tide as opposed to against it.

What other combinations or modules can we discern if we frankly open our minds and study to acquire knowledge of the possibilities?

Transfaith (Hoyle and Davies)

Through the eyes of these men, we can stand on the shoulders of all the world's thinkers and researchers and start to look out to a new greatly expanded horizon. This embraces the whole Cosmos! It behooves us to consider the concept of Intelligent Design. We cannot escape it if we contemplate the fearsome wonder of the workings of nature with its incredible biochemical and physiological machinery. What does it really mean however? We may feel, if we are honest, that it does not fit easily with the concept of a loving Personal God but more with the presence of Plato's Forms or Ideas or Blue Prints. If our life is cosmically derived by Panspermia, did that design originate in some far realm of the Cosmos? In this case, we may be separated from any guiding influence of the source of that design that might have ameliorated the harshness of our dangerous improvident environment and the lumbering course of inadequately guided evolution. In the case of man, we seem to have a blueprint which works well for about forty-five years (the life expectation about one century ago) and then leaves us high and dry with all the progressive miseries of an ailing body and failing mind (Shakespeare's Final Age)! Perhaps we can come to terms with these harsh facts surrounding our mortality through the Buddha's concepts of Impermanence and Non Attachment? By Meditation and Research, can we come to discover the true mechanism behind macro evolution? Should we not be filled with a great sense of freedom with our blank canvas with so many pictures that we may trace? The key to it all surely is the use of Mind and a sense of reverence for it combined with the great knowledge that we are part of all consciousness. Despite the woes of this tired, increasingly polluted planet, we do have a possibility of a new and exciting vision which can enable us to triumph through meditation and exploration to explore the true Reality behind our life.

A Model for Life's Journey: The Purpose-Driven Life of Rick Warren

Rick Warren is a well known tele-evangelist who has written an enormously successful book, *The Purpose-Driven Life*. The book has been so successful that Dr Warren has reimbursed all his previous salary to his church's funds. The book came particularly into the news when a young woman, Ashley Smith, was taken hostage by a murderer, Brian Nichols, who had recently killed a court judge and others. In her very hazardous situation, the young woman read to Nichols from the book. As a result of this, he finally released her and gave himself up.

In Rick Warren's analysis, the purpose-driven life has three main characteristics—I have called them the Three T's to help in remembering:

1. A Test.

We can see life with all its trials and tribulations as a test. Indeed, if one were to set out to devise a test to develop spiritual qualities and particularly the generation of compassion, one needs to look no further than life itself, with all its temptations and pitfalls. It certainly helps to find strength to stand up to all the problems that we encounter, to have this attitude—but we must *choose* it. Every experience is then of value however daunting.

2. A Trust

All of us have been endowed with certain talents and we can choose to see ourselves as trusted to use them to their maximum degree. Each of us, if we look hard enough, will find that there is some thing, or things, that we do well. We may decide to use such talents in the service of others and life itself. There is of course the biblical parable of the man who buried his talent in the earth to keep it safe and did not use it. He was chastised for his selfish action.

3. A Transience.

Life is not forever—it is transient. We have a limited time to be tested and to use our talents. The daunting fact of our mortality has been said to be the real stimulus for philosophy and religion, whereby we seek explanation and solace to help us to come to terms with this fact.

We can see the Three Ts in an existentialist way, in that we choose to view life in this way to help us superimpose a meaning or a purpose—although we must be aware of the limitations of this invention. Rick Warren, of course, would feel that this pattern is ordained by God, but we could alternatively see it as part of Intelligent Design in Hoyle's non theistic sense.

However, I must say that I found Warren's book elsewhere too fundamentalist in its viewpoint, ascribing many of mankind's problems to Eve's original transgression in the Garden of Eden. One cannot however ignore the lure of its title nor its persuasiveness.

THE PLACE FOR THEISTIC RELIGION IN A NEW WORLD VIEW: DANIEL DENNETT

Religion is an enormously important aspect of human life. Indeed we have examined the strong possibility that man is endowed with a Mystical Center (s) in his brain. Religion has been a tremendous support for man in the test of life but sadly it has been responsible for a considerable amount of evil and bigotry in the world's history. We face the possibility of a third world war superficially based on religious theistic polarization. Xenophanes in the fifth century B.C.E drew to our attention the illogicality of imaging the intelligence behind life in purely anthropomorphic form. Professor Daniel Dennett, professor of philosophy at Tufts University, deals with the problem sensitively in his current book *Breaking the Spell*. Although himself an atheist, he examines religion very fairly as a natural phenomenon:

> The research described in this book is just the beginning. Further research is needed, on both the evolutionary history of religion and on its contemporary phenomena, as they appear to different disciplines. The most pressing questions concern how we should deal with the excesses of religious upbringing and the recruitment of terrorists, but these can only be understood against a background of wider theories of religious conviction and practice. We need to secure our democratic society, the home base for this research, against the subversions of those who would use democracy as a ladder to theocracy and then throw it away, and we need to spread the knowledge that is the fruit of free inquiry. (Dennett 2006)

This is a scholarly book that sets out, in the terms of its title, to "break the spell" of discussing a subject that has hither to been taboo in many circles. It is much fairer in its treatment of this delicate subject than Richard Dawkins's book *The God Delusion* which is extremely bullish in its approach. Dennett refers to the newly coined term "bright" for an atheist, although he ponders whether this is too judgmental in its connotation. Dawkins only aims his ire at the theistic religions and, in this context, we must remember that there are at least six current non theistic world religions (Buddhism, Jainism, Confucianism, Taoism, Shinto, and Advaitic Hinduism) which represent the reality of the intelligence behind life in non anthropomorphic form.

Fred Hoyle dealt with this problem in his early book *Man and Materialism*, as follows:

> Contemporary religion is based on the religious teachings of bygone eras, often teachings that are very much older than the adherents of the modern religions realize, so old indeed that they belong to days when men understood comparatively little either about themselves or about the Universe. It was natural therefore that serious mistakes were made, mistakes that cannot survive a modern scrutiny by the rationally minded. But instead of recognizing this, contemporary religion has preferred to stick to the letter, rather than to the spirit, of the old beliefs. Faced then with outrageous contradictions it has become necessary to be increasingly vague about the meanings of the labels that describe the religious concepts. It is to be doubted whether the situation can be retrieved by an attempt to clarify the present confused situation. Rather does it seem far more

profitable to attempt to rebuild our ideas of Man's relation to the Universe from a new start, putting aside the older beliefs until some rational basis for discussing them has been achieved. (Hoyle 1957)

Hoyle's attitude does not seek to eliminate religion but to re-focus it in a way which can eliminate the embarrassing magic and myth. Man without religion is indeed a lost creature. The world's religions can be seen as great poetic works—evidence for man's search for meaning and spirituality. Man needs to be able to express reverence, or gratitude for the miracle of life. Science need not be seen as the enemy of religion but its ally demonstrating the true wonder of all that lies around us.

A COSMIC PERSPECTIVE: JOEL PRIMACK AND NANCY ABRAMS

In the last few decades, Science has progressively revealed the incredible world outside us of the Cosmos. A new book entitled *The View from the Center of the Universe* reveals this staggering world to us. It is written by a husband and wife team—he is a world renowned cosmologist and she a writer on the history and philosophy of science. The book states:

> For thousands of years, humans thought of themselves as central to the universe and created symbols and myths to make sense of the world and their special place in it. When Copernicus and Galileo shattered the view of Earth as the center of the universe, we turned away from the intuitive symbols that had sustained our ancestors, and for the past four hundred years we have seen ourselves as adrift, living on an inconsequential rock in an endless expanse of space. But recent discoveries in astronomy, physics, and cosmology have uncovered an astonishing truth: Humans actually are central to the universe in profound and important ways that derive directly from science—ways that Copernicus and Galileo could never have imagined. (Primack and Abrams, 2006)

So they are saying that the Cosmic World is accessible and meaningful and indeed we are at the center of it. This must condition our new view on life! These are the reasons that they give for saying that we are central in the cosmos:

1. We are made of the rarest material in the universe: stardust.

2. We live at the center of our Cosmic Spheres of time, because every place is the center of its own cosmic sphere of time. The finite speed of light makes this inevitable in a uniformly expanding universe.

3. We live at the midpoint of time, which is also the peak period in the entire evolution of the universe for astronomical observation.

4. We live at the middle of all possible sizes between the smallest size theoretically permitted by physics, the Planck length, and the radius of the visible universe.

5. We live in a universe that may be a rare bubble of space time in the infinite, seething cauldron of the meta-universe.

6. We live at more or less the midpoint in the life of our planet and also at the midpoint of the best period for complex life on our planet.

7. We live at a turning point for our species.

We need to digest mentally all of this new information to derive a new meaningful view of life.

Nancy Abrams kindly checked the above material when I sent e-mail copies of this book to all the living authors and she made some necessary corrections. She did however also make the comment, "You might want to rethink the manuscript's extremely male-orientated selection of views on the meaning of life." It really shook me to realize that only two female thinkers are mentioned! I can only respond by saying that I am a feminist and that the two individuals cited are both extremely effective and vocal proponents of the all important female voices in philosophy, science and religion. Nancy Abrams does point out forcefully that her and Joel Primack's aim is a "scientifically chosen view of life which is nevertheless meaningful. It is not religious." I thank her for putting me right.

A NEW ETHIC: COSMIC COMPASSIONATE PLURALITY

If we were trying to postulate a new basis for a religious approach to life, what elements would we choose? From the basis of all that we have learned from the lives described, let us make an attempt! Our new life may be chosen to be:

1. Cosmic.

We must take in all the new knowledge of the Cosmos—it is our domain and our heritage. It must condition our life view.

2. Compassionate.

We have learned that Compassion is the Golden Rule behind all the World Religions. Sadly, the world is full of suffering and the only conceivable justification for suffering, inadequate though it maybe, is that it acts as a cue for Compassion. Many other words may be used for compassion such as Agape, Koruna, Selfless Love but the meaning is always the same, being ultimate active concern for the well being of all sentient beings.

3. Pluralistic.

A new attitude can set out to extend our compassion to the plurality of all of the world's religions and all those who are not yet able to see the world in a religious sense. Somehow we must develop spiritually to allow us to do this. It could be possible that other factors may come into play to make this happen. For example if extraterrestrial life is discovered in the future this may force us to see ourselves as one species when we come to interrelate with life elsewhere.

So I have entitled this ethic Cosmic, Compassionate, Plurality. Obviously, it is only a small start in our search for a new identity.

WHERE NOW? THE JOY OF LIVING, YONGEY MINGYUR AND DANIEL GOLEMAN

The most basic of all human aims is to achieve Happiness. If it is an unselfish happiness then it must be a legitimate goal in any new attitude to life. Aristotle answered the question "What is the good life for man?" by stating "It is a life of happiness." In his work *Nicomachean Ethics* Aristotle defines what he means by "happiness": "Happiness is an activity of the soul in accord with perfect virtue. (Aristotle, *Nicomachean Ethics*)

He said that you may tell a good man because he is a happy man. We must therefore achieve goodness in our cosmic, compassionate plurality. *The Joy of Living. Unlocking the Secret and Science of Happiness*, by Yongey Mingyur and Daniel Goleman, is a bestseller. This is a Buddhist text and explores the role of meditation in our search for happiness and even more joy. It reviews the growing field of brain monitoring in relation to mindfulness.

There is no doubt that this is a time for deep reflection on the part of the human species. We are heirs to so much information and science. We may be mindful of Teilhard de Chardin's concept of the Thinking Noosphere. We are being drawn closer and closer together in a communicative network. As a conscious species, we have the enormous privilege to be part of mind. We need to think our way through the concept of the mind of the universe, of which we are a part. We are indeed at the center of the universe and its very nature. If we gently and reverently put the theistic religions on one side for the moment, it is possible that we may be capable of thinking ourselves towards a clearer concept of the intelligence behind all life.

GARY SCHWARTZ AND WILLIAM SIMON WITH G.O.D. AS GUIDING ORGA-NIZING DESIGNING PROCESS

Gary Schwartz

Gary Schwartz and William Simon in their recent book *The G.O.D. Experiments* explain G.O.D. as Guiding, Organizing, Designing Process! He states:

> Imagine that G.O.D. is literally inside you right now, patiently waiting for you to wake up to this inner ultimate reality. Are you ready to wake up? (Schwartz and Simon, 2006)

The human race is already waking up to a new era. Look at the titles of the books that have just been cited. Gandhi said that truth is God, and the Buddha is quoted as saying at the end of his life, when he achieved Para nirvana: "Be a light unto yourselves." We can go forward in the truth to experience the true selfless, unfettered joy of living.

Answer: We may attempt an ethic of Cosmic, Compassionate Plurality.

Reading List and Sources

The Purpose Driven Life. Rick Warren. Zondervan, 2002.

Breaking The Spell. Daniel Dennett. Viking. 2006.

The View From the Center of the Universe. Joel Primack and Nancy Ellen Abrams. Riverhead Books 2006.

The Joy of Living. Yongey Mingyur Rinpoche and Daniel Goleman. Harmony Books 2007.

The G.O.D.Experiments. Gary Schwartz and William Simon. Atria Books. 2006.

CHAPTER 14. MEDITATION AS A MEANS TO MEANING

Shakespeare And Stuart Kauffman Together With David Comings

Question: Can Meditation and Debate bring us to new
depths of meaning and a new sense of the sacred?

THE LOSS OF MAGIC AND MYTH

Shakespeare: The Tempest (Act V, Epilogue): Prospero:
"Now my charms are all o'erthrown,
And what strength I have's mine own,
Which is most faint."

Prospero, perhaps Shakespeare's archetype of divinity in his enchanted island, in that magical apparently farewell play "The Tempest," relinquishes his magical powers in order to return to normal life by breaking his magic staff and drowning his book of spells in the ocean. He has to emerge in his own strength. Shakespeare himself was facing retirement in his early fifties due to ill health (he would be dead in three years). He was to leave the frenetic bustle of London and return to the countryside of Stratford as a prosperous land owner but to face up to the apparent unhappiness of his marriage to Anne Hathaway—it had been an enforced union when she became pregnant at age 26 and he was only 19. His great tragedy, "King Lear," featuring the king's stormy renunciation of his crown and division of his kingdom appears also to have been written as Shakespeare contemplated his own change of circumstances. Significantly, the play is set in ancient, pagan Britain, avoiding current religious issues—again Shakespeare was keeping his head down metaphorically. Like Prospero, he would sacrifice his own magic as a playwright, and like Lear would have to make painful choices in his last will and testament, leaving only the second-best bed to his wife and virtually all else to his favorite daughter Susannah. It was a transformation as great as that which confronts modern man or woman as they emerge from the protective myth and magic of realist theistic religion into a new era marked by their own strength. This strength also may appear "most faint" until the newly emerged realize that a profound metamorphosis has taken place. Their greatest strength lies in their possession of mind with its potent meditative function and their link with the intelligence of the cosmos.

ISVARA as a Symbol of Meditative Inspiration and Jung's God Archetype as the Self

Interestingly, Mircea Eliade in his previously-cited monograph on yoga mentions that a new non-creationist god archetype, Isvara, had been reported by Patananjali, the great chronicler of yoga techniques, as being capable of arising in the consciousness of the Yogin (meditator) to hasten his deliverance:

Isvara...is, of course, no creator (the cosmos, life, and man, as we already noted had, been "created" by prakriti, for they all proceed from the primordial substance). But in the case of certain men, Isvara can hasten the process of deliverance; he helps them towards a more speedy arrival at Samadhi. (Eliade, 1990)

One is mindful of Jung's insight that the Self represents the god archetype deep within us—archetype being defined as "imprint." Isvara could be interpreted as a symbol of this archetypal structure. One must be mindful that the Buddhist bodhisattva Avalokitesvara, who symbolizes compassion (he who hears the cries of the world), has "svara" compounded into his name. The illustration shows the prayer wheel presented by the Dalai Lama to Nova Southeastern University, where I work; it is housed in our Library.

Within its structure are myriads of copies of the mantra to Avalokiteshvara: "Om Mane Padme Hum." Every time that the wheel is spun, this message is believed to be dispatched out into the cosmos to plead for compassion to all sentient beings.

INTRODUCING STUART KAUFFMAN AND "REINVENTING THE SACRED"

It was only after writing the main substance of this work that I found mention of Stuart Kauffman's latest book published in 2008, which I have read avidly finding much of relevance to our frank pursuit for meaning in its brilliant but somewhat difficult exposition. He is truly a return to the pattern of the Renaissance Man who could span multiple disciplines in his knowledge. He currently holds joint appointments as a professor in the University of Calgary in the fields of Biological Sciences, Physics, Astronomy and Philosophy—what a combination of backgrounds for us to tap! I should also add, that he originally trained as a medical doctor! He dedicates his book to "conversations we must have"—well, conversations are really a form of joint meditation? The train of his thought can be discerned from the titles of previous works:

- *Origins of Order: Self-Organization and Selection in Evolution*, 1993.
- *At Home in the Universe*, 1995.
- *Investigations*, 2000.

Amazingly, he is a prominent scientist who states that scientific algorithms, particle physics and reductionism are unable to explain much of the mysteries of life. Listen to this extract: "I will demonstrate the inadequacy of reductionism. Even major physicists now doubt its full legitimacy. I shall show that biology and its evolution cannot be reduced to physics alone but stand in their own right." (Kauffman, 2008)

He claims that life and with it agency come naturally to exist in the universe. He states that with agency came values, meaning, and doing, all of which are as real in the universe as particles in motion. "Real," for him, here has a particular meaning. While life, agency, value, and doing presumably have physical explanations in any specific organism, the evolutionary emergence of these cannot be derived from or reduced to physics alone. Thus life, agency, value, and doing are real in the universe. This stance he calls emergence.

So he recognizes the existence of values again after their virtual eclipse in the aftermath of existentialism and post modernism. So called agency emerges from nature mysteriously and values are an inevitable accompaniment. Even at the most elementary level of a bacterium swimming up a glucose gradient to obtain food, without attributing consciousness, Kauffman sees in this capacity the evolutionary onset of choice and thus of meaning, value, doing and purpose. Darwinian evolution cannot be reduced to physics, he states—it is not possible to write down the laws of evolution of the biosphere. The complexity of biological systems and organisms might result just as well from self-organization and far—from-equilibrium dynamics as from Darwinian natural selection—he proposes the first models of Boolean genetic networks. He seriously doubts the power and sufficiency of natural selection as the sole motor of evolution.

Kauffman is a secular humanist but is reluctant to abandon the term God altogether as he recognizes its huge historical role in mankind's development. He has no place for a creator God but instead suggests retaining the term God in a non anthropomorphic sense for the very creativity of the universe. This creativity produces the often unpredictable emergence of all life forms but also the features of our culture including economics, law and art. It provides us with a new sense of the sacred and a need for faith in the process. This, we may reflect, creates a form of pantheism or more truly monism to be compared to that of the philosopher Spinoza in the seventeenth century, which led to his ostracism by religious authority. Fortunately we live in more tolerant times where it is possible to examine such provocative concepts. Indeed Kauffman's idea is a potent stimulus to thought! Pantheism views God in a non-anthropomorphic sense as equating with nature and the universe as opposed to Panentheism where nature and the universe are a part of god. Deism conceives a god who sets the universe in being but then plays no further active role with it (Aristotle's unmoved mover). On the other hand, Pan deism combines the concepts of Deism and Pantheism with a god who creates the universe and then becomes it. All of these alternatives are great subjects for meditative contemplation.

Is it cheating a little, to retain the word God in these contexts, or in that of Gary Schwartz with his G.O.D. (Guiding, Organizing, Designing Process)? Could we not use the term Intelligence or Mind, avoiding anthropomorphism? By the way, Kauffman disparages the concept of intelligent design on the grounds that it is fundamentalist biblical creationism. This is certainly not so if we go back to Fred Hoyle as its original, largely forgotten or cast aside, proponent.

Kauffman's View of Buddhism

Kauffman has respect for Buddhism as an important example of non-theistic religion:

> What more do we really need of a God, if we also accept that we, at last, are responsible to the best of our forever-limited wisdom. What we are discussing here is also similar in many ways to Buddhism, a wisdom tradition without a God, based on thousands of years of investigation into consciousness. Because Buddhism does not hold to a Creator God and is a way of life, with deep understanding of our emotional-rational-intuitive selves, I would hope that the rest of us have much to learn from its years of study of human consciousness. If we must understand our humanity, wisdom suggests that we use all the resources that we can find. (Kauffman, 2008)

The Theory of Forms/Archetypes Revisited in the Context of Intelligent Design

Kauffman brings to our attention the great mystery of the creativity of the universe which he, as an eminent scientist, says is not fully predictable by known laws or Darwinian natural selection. This creativity is responsible for the emergence of the extraordinary richness of the natural world, the complex spheres of our political, economic and legal existence together with the great variety of artistic expression. It creates agency, and with it, values and meaning. He wishes to enshrine it as our alternative god figure while an alternative, I suggest, is simply to use the term cosmic intelligence for it—the great innate mind of the universe. We can certainly feel it to be sacred in its awesome power and beauty and an object of prayers of thanks and wonder. We must resist the temptation to give it an anthropomorphic face, although if we ourselves are an integral part of creation it is not inconceivable that it could assume such a human-like form if need be. Remember Xenophanes and the horses that would be likely to draw gods like horses. Remember Hoyle with his reflections that an underlying intelligence could take some unsuspected form, even gaseous. We need to think and meditate outside the box.

Does this creativity work totally unscripted or is there a hidden scenario written in a medium as yet uncovered by our science? Did Plato and Socrates intuit something of this by contemplation when they proposed a system of Forms (or Blue Prints in more modern parlance) and did Jung, through his mystical introversion, discover one facet in his concept of the Archetypes?

The history of the search for so called universals has been a recurrent one in philosophy, although it was suppressed by voices in the era of Scholasticism, that period when Christianity dominated philosophic thought, such as Abelard (1079–1142) and William of Ockham (1290–1349), lest this concept might be seen to limit an anthropomorphic God's options. It is rather different, however, if we view this as a statement of the options themselves. The current school of intelligent design can be viewed as a modern attempt to bring science itself into the search and emphatically not a back tracking as a ploy to bring back the creationist God of Genesis. Rupert Sheldrake's intuitive ideas of morphic resonance and morphic fields are also relevant.

How are the blueprints written? Not in the forms of tablets of stone or plates of gold as in religion of old, although one should not deride these human attempts to express the truth in mythical form. They seem to be encoded into the very substance of nature in the genome and the Boolean networks that Kauffman studies, and possibly in morphic fields. We know that a single skin cell has all the information to reproduce the whole body, but even that startling fact is only a part of a great sacred miracle. Parts of the blue prints are incorporated into the very warp and weft of the fabric of life itself. Hoyle pondered the possibility of Intelligence being imbedded in the substance of life itself as well as remotely. We may remember that Mircea Eliade spoke of the sacrality of nature in his study of all the world's religions—it is sacred and we are sacred.

Kauffman repeatedly refers to Plato and the Forms. He points out that we cannot know fully, but must live our lives anyway so that we live forward into mystery: "Our deep need is to better understand how we do so, and to learn from this deep feature of life how to live our lives well. Plato said we seek the Good, the True, and the Beautiful. Plato points us in the right direction." (Kauffman, 2008)

That's quite something when a fifth century B.C.E. rationalist philosopher can provide inspiration to a third millennium scientist—shades of Whitehead's famous statement that all Western philosophy is footnotes to Plato.

DAVID COMINGS: MAKING OUR SPIRITUAL
BRAIN AT PEACE WITH OUR THINKING BRAIN

David Comings is a polymath like Stuart
Kauffman being a physician, neuroscientist,
behavioral and molecular geneticist of emi-
nence. He is a past president of the American
Society of Human Genetics. From this wide
background of experience, his viewpoint is
that of a sensitive, compassionate atheist. He
expounds his views in his 2008 book *Did Man Create God*. His conclusion is,
"The evidence suggests that our rational brain created God to satisfy the
transcendent yearnings of our spiritual brain. Instead of denying the existence and reality of the spiritual brain, we need to provide for an accommo-
dation between rationality and spirituality, a way for them to live together
in peaceful co-existence. . . . Both historically and logically Ockham's razor
suggests that the poetic and inspirational verses of the Bible and other holy
books were...written by poetic and inspirational humans." (Comings, 2008)

This is a scholarly and brilliant exposition, which reads like a scientific
textbook with copious references to back up its propositions. Man is clearly a religious animal but what can be a religion for someone who uses logic
and science in his or her reasoning? This is the critical point of his book and
indeed of this present work. Comings pleads for "a rational spirituality" as
does Kauffman and as do I! Which faiths meet his requirements?—Secular Humanism, Buddhism and Jainism while Unitarianism, Reform Judaism and Taoism are compatible with minor qualifications. Well, that is a
good start providing material for honest debate and meditation! The only
question that Comings does not tackle is how it came to pass that a species should arise that has the intelligence to seek its origins and that is endowed with a myth making faculty to create provisional explanations like
anthropomorphic god (s) to strive to find some meaning in life. May not
this be part of the Intelligent Design that lies as a blue print for sentient life?
Dr Comings would part company with me here as he equates Intelligent
Design with Theistic Creationism, but I would respectfully ask him to consider Hoyle's concept of non—anthropomorphic Intelligence as a debating
topic!

Our Purpose Here

If we are conscious of a Purpose in our life, it automatically provides a meaning. We then require our gifted days to enable us to carry out that purpose. It may be that we already feel that Purpose. However, most of us seem to crave purpose. Look at the phenomenal success of Rick Warren's book *The Purpose-Driven Life*—I suggest that it is the title firstly that draws people to it. If we lack a purpose, where can we find one? One cardinal way is to look for a problem that needs to be addressed. What is the greatest problem that the world currently faces? In very general terms, it can be summarized as Suffering, in all its multiple forms, affecting all sentient beings. The Buddhist faces this uncompromisingly, as one of the most important components of his or her required eight fold path is Right Occupation. One's occupation or work should allow one to express the central tenets of benevolence, compassion, joy in the joy of others and equanimity—an approach to Suffering. The only good thing to emerge from Suffering is surely that it is a cue for Compassion—the golden rule which is the ethical core of all the world's great religions. I am fortunate in my work as a doctor to be able to feel a direct link to the alleviation of suffering if I attempt to work selflessly and with energy. All occupations, however, if undertaken compassionately and caringly, reduce the world's load of suffering and have this meaningful link. Most people find that a compassionate act makes them feel right inside, making it possible that consciousness of the form of the Good is built into us all if we open ourselves to it.

Boredom

Boredom is an ever present hazard in modern life, robbing us of the rewards of interest and satisfaction in life's tasks. I am sure that Plato would have cited Knowledge as the prime antidote to boredom. New learning spurs the mind into activity, and interest springs forth. The creativity and emergence that Kauffman speaks of are constantly stirring the pot of life to bring more to our contemplation. He points out that we can never predict precisely what will arise in what he calls the adjacent present so that there is a built in excitement to provide zest. One major incitement to boredom lies in the all too prevalent tendency, particularly in commerce, to create jobs which lack human interest and satisfaction. To make matters worse, such posts are often accompanied by the tedium of endless form filling and unnecessary interpersonal stress. Those of us who have the privilege of having others working under us, in a common task, have a duty to design their work plan to provide balance, interest and satisfaction and to disseminate a feeling of happiness with benevolence in the work place. It is not easy, of course, but it is a purpose in its own right with its own significant rewards. Recreation is an all important aspect. The word itself indicates that we have the possibility to re-create or re-make ourselves by what we do in our spare time. Let us remember that Winston Churchill was advised that he needed a potent hobby when he was confronted with the frustration and potential boredom of lying fallow politically. Painting was his solution and he records how this opened his mind to the miracles of light and nature and transformed him. Painting is the only art where the practitioner can start to produce meaningful and satisfying results almost at once! That is providing he or she paints or draws what they feel about an object rather than working to please. This is expressionism, an important contribution of modern art: remember that children produce wonderfully vivid art because they create emotionally as they feel. They paint a human being with a large head because our head is our most important part and so it is! All of the Arts have the ability to lift us to a different plane as Schopenhauer pointed out in his perceived escape from the tyranny of the Will. Churchill also had recourse to writing. I am writing now trapped in bed with an injured leg propped up in front of me under a mountain of ice—it is enormously therapeutic to write. It is said we all have at least one book inside us and I believe it. What about all that background knowledge that we need for such a task? I have my lab top in my lap and have access in a moment to the staggering variety of information that mankind has amassed by calling up one of many search engines—although Google is sufficient for the majority of needs. Reading, of course, is a recreation that is the compliment of writing. Baron de Montesquieu, the eighteenth century French writer, said that there is no problem on earth which is not made easier by an hour with a good book. I believe this and always have a book in my brief case. I am easily fatigued but by short bouts of reading several times a day one can often get through a book in a week—I strongly recommend this dipping method! A word of caution is to distinguish true recreations from mere pastimes to obtain maximum benefit.

The Final Oblivion of Death: Paraeschaton and Eschaton

Shakespeare in his seven ages of man makes the last stage that of "oblivion," with loss of mental and physical faculties. Shakespeare uses the personage of Jacques in "As You Like It," however, to express a rather jaundiced image with no reference to a possible afterlife as the Protestant faith holding sway during his mature life would have had him believe. In this context, let us recall the wonderfully pragmatic approach of Socrates, who felt that there were two acceptable alternatives after this life, namely nothing, in the form of the Big Sleep, as he termed it humorously, or alternatively an existence after death in which he would welcome the possibility of engaging great thinkers of previous eras (perhaps testing them with his dialectical approach?). The Buddha was more non-committal, regarding knowledge of such matters (the Avyacata) as unnecessary to live a good life. Don Cupitt, who featured in our Introduction, cautioned us to remember that there is no scientific evidence for life after death, so that we must live this present one fully and exuberantly, as expounded in his book *Life, Life*.

What should we make of these disparate views? It is a telling factor in defining meaning behind our existence, even if the Buddha indicated that, in his time, it was inappropriate to pry too deeply. Maybe, with more data to evaluate, we might be excused for wishing to peer more deeply behind the veil. John Hick, our Inter Faith authority, has pointed out that all the major religions have a cosmic optimism that all will ultimately be well. He divides discussion into the Paraeschaton, shortly after death, and the Eschaton, as our ultimate fate (basing this on the Greek word *eschata* for last things). He points out that the Eastern faiths such as Hinduism and Buddhism have a basically horizontal concept of a wheel of future lives lived on this earth (Samsara) as a result of Karma, our past deeds, as opposed to the vertical concept of the three great Abrahamic faiths of a future abode in a heavenly site or alternatively in a subterranean Hell, depending again on our deeds and perceived "sins." We may infer that the bulk of humanity has chosen to take a view of a continuing existence, although we may question whether this could be wish fulfillment to calm the fear of non-being. John Hick comments that we may be on safer ground if we confine discussion to the Paraeschaton. Some might consider the abundant data on the near death experience as possible evidence that intelligent design has incorporated this as our final experience of this life as an instance of compassion built into that blue print.

The Near Death Experience (NDE) and
The Tibetan Book of the Dead

Many thousands of instances of the NDE have now been reported by subjects who have recovered after being very close to death due to such hazards as cardiac arrest, drowning or falling from mountains. The stages of this may be (it is variable in its extension):

- Feelings of Peace
- Out of Body Sensation
- Tunnel of Darkness
- Brilliant Light
- Being of Light
- Life Review
- Barrier
- Another Wonderful Country
- Meeting Deceased Loved Ones
- Point of Decision
- The Return
- Profound Aftermath

Not all of these elements may occur in a particular case, and there are cultural differences in the components. In very occasional instances the experience may be unpleasant, but for the majority it is profoundly moving, bringing many uncommitted people to a religious outlook and obliterating any future fear of death. Attempts have been made to explain these manifestations as merely due to physical factors such as the doctor's ophthalmoscope shining in the eye or the effects of reduced oxygen or raised carbon dioxide on the failing brain. These objections have been dismissed one by one by Dr Peter Fenwick, a distinguished English neuropsychiatrist, in the book he wrote with his wife entitled *The Truth In The Light*. He has decided firmly that the NDE is a mystical phenomenon. Dr Persinger claims that components of the NDE can be elicited by magneto-metric stimulation of the right temporo-parietal area—the postulated Mystical Center of the brain. Intelligent design could have endowed us with this faculty to benignly round off our life. Shakespeare may be expressing some intuition of this in Prospero's moving invocation:

The cloud-capp'd towers, the gorgeous palaces,
The solemn temples, the great globe itself,
Yea, all which it inherit, shall dissolve
And like this insubstantial pageant faded,
Leave not a rack behind. We are such stuff
As dreams are made on; and our little life
Is rounded with a sleep. ("The Tempest." Act III, Scene 3)

Shakespeare reduces the impact of his cruel final Oblivion rounding it or softening it with an unspecified sleep—and so may intelligent design. Should we ask for more, in the form of a fully developed Eschaton, where we might exist for an eternity in some ethereal form? Have we not been privileged to know a life on this earth? Anyway, how could such a future kingdom be organized to accommodate the trillions of departed souls—the possibilities for endless new suffering and boredom loom large without some inspired choreography.

I look at the birds in all their beauty and ask myself whether they might have an after-life. The answer to me is clearly "No," and I wonder why we are so presumptuous as to feel that we, as human beings, deserve preservation into perpetuity, save for the works we have left behind—though the occasional saint or genius might be worthy of more? Should we not be grateful if we have a final farewell event in the form of the NDE? It seems to be personally designed, because it is peopled with our own religious icons, as the cultural differences between East and West show. In our mystical center, we appear to have a database similar to the "my pictures" folder in our PC ("my sacred pictures"), which obediently spills out its contents at our final demise to provide us with a personal life review and a sensed presence of our predilection and companions of our choice.

The features of the Bardo Land as described in the *Tibetan Book of the Dead*, dating from around 8th century Tibetan Buddhism, have some intriguing features in common with the NDE, particularly the intense bright light and a life review. If the departed has the courage to follow that particular light, he or she may escape the endless toil of Samsara, the Wheel of Life, to achieve the great and merciful void of Sunyata—envisioned by some as a mighty quantum field and repository of energy. The Book is at pains to point out that the personages we meet in the Bardo, such as Benign and Wrathful deities, are the creations of our own minds.

Inspiration from Nature

In the NDE, individuals may emerge from the tunnel of light into a landscape which fills them with a sense of wonder and beauty so that they do not want to leave. One is reminded of Plato's intimation that the true Forms behind life are so much more vivid than their earthly counterparts and indeed his concept of anamnesis, whereby learning is remembering our experience in some other sphere of existence. These are mysteries worthy of subjects for meditation.

There is so much to learn from contemplating nature. Let us take another quotation from Shakespeare:

> And this our life, exempt from public haunt,
> Finds tongues in trees, books in the running brooks,
> Sermons in stones, and good in everything.
> (Duke Senior, "As You Like It." Act II, Scene 1)

There are indeed tongues in the trees and books in the brooks not to mention the sermons in stones if we can but attune ourselves to their messages. Shakespeare was talking of his local beloved Forest of Arden—I know its location well in my home county of Warwickshire. I find similar inspiration in my new home of Florida with its extraordinary juxtaposition of exotic sub-tropical plants and trees from all over the world, which I view with wonder on my bird watching walks not to mention the miraculous birds themselves. Shakespeare had a great eye for the natural world doubtless derived from his contact with the rural world of Warwickshire and expressed his reactions in wonderfully memorable prose and poetry. Fred Hoyle loved to hill walk in the Lake District but his fertile mind probed further to detect possibilities of cosmic genes in what he saw. For example, he conjectured that Chlorophyll, the green pigment of the plant world, was likely to be an interstellar molecule pointing out the similarities of its light absorbing properties to interstellar dust. Hoyle found great inspiration in the music of Beethoven, who routinely wandered in the countryside while composing as if transcribing from nature itself—as did Brahms. Mircea Eliade spoke of the sacrality of nature.

Meaning

We have been fishing for meaning in the deep and mysterious seas of life! Is the net empty as Don Cupitt would predict it would be from his vantage point in a long chain of reductionist philosophers dating back to the Existentialists? Does the net have a large rent in its belly, allowing any capture to escape because we have trolled somewhat heretical waters full of hidden snags as the religious realists would expect? Those of you who have had the tenacity to stay with me on the blustery trip will, I hope, have been presented with enough material by our Thinkers to make your own assessment of the catch. There are many fish glistening in the confines of the net. Let us give them some names—obviously this has to be something of an individual credo as each of us must ultimately decide for him or her self:

• We live in a fascinating world of constant emergence; boredom should be unknown to us.

• With agency, meaning and value come automatically.

• Intelligent design in nature must surely be apparent to us if we delve into structure and function.

• We need to use all our faculties to pursue and intuit the form of that intelligence in relation to its location, its history and its intentionality towards us as this will deepen our sense of ultimate meaning.

• Nature itself should be brought back into prominence as our Inspiration so that we feel its sacrality.

• We must persevere to comprehend the full development of our four part brain to understand the factors favoring evolution rather than devolution of our nervous systems.

• We must understand our possibility for transcendence in a social sense avoiding the hold of culture alone.

• Let us revere the world's great religions as poetic monuments to man's impassioned search for meaning but not lack in courage to go beyond them in a search for the way to cosmic, compassionate plurality devoid of shame and coercion as of old.

• We may feel the need to try to image the intelligence and mind behind life in new forms realizing the limitations of many anthropomorphic images of existing religions.

• We may wish to explore new forms of prayer to express thanks, awe and reverence but not expecting a personal intervention on our part. We must grow up to stand with the rest of nature on our own two feet giving thanks for our independence.

• Let us meditate and converse on these ultimate matters.

• We never need to abandon a religious attitude to the miracle of life but only to grow in our imagery and understanding.

Answer: What strength we have is our own, but we have the inestimable privilege of linking with the Intelligence of our Universe—what greater meaning can we ask?

Reading List and Sources

Reinventing The Sacred. Stuart Kauffman. Basic Books, 2008

Did Man Create God? David Comings. Hope Press, 2008.

The Truth In The Light. Peter Fenwick and Elizabeth Fenwick. Headline Book Publishing 1995.

CHAPTER 15. A POSTSCRIPT ON EVOLUTION
AS A GUIDE TO ULTIMATE MEANING

JERRY COYNE, RICHARD DAWKINS AND DAVID COMINGS

The Challenge: "Reading the Braille" of Evolution

Paul MacLean, the neuroscientist whose theory of the Triune Brain was quoted in Chapter 8, stated provocatively: "And so, one might conclude we are left with the question as to whether or not there can ever evolve an intelligence that will be intelligent enough to take measure of itself and at the same time discover a Braille for reading the blind message of evolution." (MacLean, 1990).

The year 2009 marked the 150th anniversary of Darwin's *The Origin of Species* and, as might be expected, it spawned a host of books setting out to summarize the present status of the theory of evolution, notably those by Richard Dawkins in England and his American counterpart Jerry Coyne, together with a remarkable color atlas entitled *Prehistoric Life*, commissioned by the publishers Dorling Kindersley from an international team of paleontological experts. These are powerful works setting out the current knowledge relating to our search for the meaning of what it is to be human—at the end of what is claimed to be the incredibly long trail of life on this planet, 3.5 billion years. The title of Coyne's impressive book *Why Evolution Is True* makes the claim for the absolute validity of the theory, and the facts are now very impressive, as all can read for themselves. But is it all a "blind message" or can we start to lift the veil and see the truth, as with Plato's man in the cave who broke free to come face to face with the light? Then we may hope to acquire the intelligence to "take measure" of ourselves.

Looking Down the Vast Corridors of Time

What an enormity of time we are bidden to contemplate! Can we take it all in? Let us briefly summarize the 14 previous periods of living matter:

- Archaen: −2.5 billion years ago. After the Great Cometary Bombardment comes the advent of very simple single non nucleated organisms, the prokaryotes, such as Strombolites.
- Proterozoic: 2.5 billion–542 million. The entry of nucleated eukaryotes, bacteria and archea, plus simple animals and plants.
- Cambrian: 542–488 m. An explosion of life forms predating all ensuing phyla as evidenced in the Burgess Shale.
- Ordovician: 490–440 m. Arthropods appear; extinctions of various life forms take place.
- Silurian: 440–410 m. The first fishes and vascular plants.
- Devonian: 410–350 m. The age of fishes and an expansion of plant growth that makes the earth green
- Carboniferous: 359–300 m. Tree ferns multiply (the origin of eventual coal deposits).
- Permian: 300–258 m. Mass extinction of 90 per cent of vertebrate species. A great Ice Age.
- Triassic: 250–200 m. Dinosaurs appear, together with small mammals. Pterosaurs introduce flight.

• Jurassic: 200–140 m. Dinosaurs and flying reptiles. Gingko trees. Dragon flies. Amphibia.

• Cretaceous: 140–70 m. Greenhouse high temperatures. Pinnacle of dinosaur life. Archaeopteryx.

• Paleogene: 70–20 m. Development of mammal species.

• Neogene: 25–2 m. Ice Age. The formation of Grasslands.

• Quaternary: 2–0.5 m. Hominid life.

What an extraordinary chronicle of time. How can we assimilate it all? Is there an underlying pattern? Certainly we can discern a process whereby simple life forms progressively achieve increasing complexity.

Is Evolution Blind or Is There an Underlying Blueprint or a Recipe?

In Dawkin's book *The Greatest Show on Earth*, he sets out to bring together his ideas on evolution. In the chapter entitled "You Did It Yourself In Nine Months," he points out that we can witness the stages of the increasing complexity involved in evolution when we observe the development of a human fetus, through the apparent forms of fish to amphibian to reptile to mammal—"ontogeny recapitulating phylogeny" in the somewhat discredited phraseology of the German evolutionist and Darwin's contemporary Ernst Haeckel. Dawkins departs from his usual matter of fact pragmatism occasionally as when he states that animal bodies are "so beautifully put together that it seems impossible to believe that the genes that program their development don't function as a blue print, a design ,a master plan" However he comes to the conclusion that these do not exist but there could be instead "a recipe" as follows:

> A recipe captures something of the truth and it is an analogy that I sometimes use, to explain why "blueprint" is not appropriate. Unlike a blueprint a recipe is irreversible. If you follow a cake recipe step by step, you will end up with a cake. But you can't take a cake and reconstruct the recipe—certainly not the exact words of the recipe—whereas, as we have seen, you could take a house and reconstruct something close to the original blueprint. (Dawkins, 2009)

A blueprint, he points out, uses a top-down process whereas a recipe uses a bottom-up function where all is done by local rules utilizing in this case "self assembly." Now Dawkins is discussing embryology but we might extrapolate to conclude that there could be a recipe behind evolution itself. A recipe requires an intelligence to devise it in the normal way, we may surmise, although Dawkins would part company with us at that point, I am sure!

The Apparent Cruelty of the Evolutionary
Process: Nature Red in Tooth and Claw?

The poet Alfred Lord Tennyson in his poem "In Memoriam A.H.H." in 1850, in the time of Darwin, put it like this, as Coyne reminds us:

> [Man] Who trusted God was love indeed
> And love Creation's final law—
> Tho' Nature red in tooth and claw
> With ravine shrieked against his creed.

At first sight the whole evolutionary process does appear so incredibly prolonged and harsh under the rigors of Natural Selection that it is hard to discern a caring empathy and indeed Tennyson proposes a rift between Creation's inherent love and Nature's actual performance. This has the feel of Plato's Deity who entrusted the practicalities of fashioning the natural world to a Demiurge who may have not followed his initial intent! Must we feel such a dualism? Let us listen to Schopenhauer with his Buddhist viewpoint:

> All these (creatures), provided with little foresight, go about guilelessly among the dangers that threaten their existence every moment. Since now nature exposes its organisms, constructed with such inimitable skill, not only to the predatory instincts of the stronger, but also to the blindest chance...it declares that the annihilation of these individuals is indifferent to it...It says this very distinctly and does not lie...If now the all-mother sends forth her children without protection to a thousand threatening dangers this can only be because she knows that, if they fall, they fall back into her womb where they are safe; therefore their fall is a mere jest. (Schopenhauer 1818)

This implies that things are not as cruel as they may appear at first sight. One is reminded of David Livingstone, the Victorian explorer of South Africa—as a minister and doctor he was appalled at the apparent brutality of the natural world about him where he saw animals such as antelopes suffering from the actions of predators such as lions. How could his Loving God allow such a thing? While he was musing over this difficult problem in theodicy, a very seminal event occurred as recorded in lithographs of the period! He was in the African bush when suddenly a lion leapt upon him, impaling his arm with such ferocity that his humerus was shattered. This was established when his body was examined years later, at his death; a malunion of the bone was discovered. He would have perished if a bearer had not appeared, at the last moment, to shoot the lion. After this disturb-ing event, an extraordinary realization came to Livingstone. He had not felt any pain at the time of his injury, and moreover, everything seemed to slow down so that he experienced no fear. Livingstone came to the momentous conclusion that this must also be the situation with the predated animal—His God was not so cruel after all! Indeed it is common knowledge that a soldier, under the stress of battle, may have a limb blown off without feeling pain, at the time. The physiological mechanism is now known in that the anterior pituitary gland in the brain produces a substance called Proprio-cortin which is broken down into beta-endorphin, a potent analgesic agent, related to opium and morphine, which floods the bloodstream. Indeed, Liv-ingstone is certain to have had laudanum, a form of opium, derived from the poppy, in his medical bag. The all-mother, personifying nature, is more merciful than it appears on the surface.

The Formation of Species:
Darwin is Reticent, for Once!

The engine of evolution is natural selection—so says Darwin and so say Coyne and Dawkins. Man may imitate it with artificial selection—here de-sired varieties are produced by planned breeding to meet the breeder's de-sires rather than the dictates of the natural environment. Sexual selection is another possibility whereby the preference of the female governs which male mates with her to pass on his genes. Alternatively so called genetic drift may occasionally operate which "occurs by random sampling of dif-ferent alleles (a particular form of a given gene produced by mutation) from one generation to the next—this causes non adaptive evolutionary change." All of these mechanisms variously explain microevolution in which certain naturally occurring variations in a species, with underlying genetic muta-tions, cause changes in the traits of the members of the species because they aid survival or satisfy the desires of the breeder or the taste of the mate or occur randomly.

However, what about macroevolution which Coyne defines as "large changes in body form or the evolution of one type of plant or animal from another."? In other words it relates to the formation of a new species—so called speciation. Firstly, how are we told that one species can be differenti-ated from another—there are three ways :

• Morphological Species Concept (MSC)

A group of individuals that resemble each other more than they resemble members of other groups. Thus we can distinguish a cat from a dog on the basis of many different traits. It is the sort of classification that was pioneered by Linnaeus in the eighteenth century (a doctor who converted to natural history).

• Biological Species Concept (BSC)

A group of inter-breeding natural populations that are reproductively isolated from other such groups. This is a much less subjective criterion. If individuals can mate with each other and produce living offspring then they belong to the same species. This cannot apply to bacteria which reproduce asexually.

• Genetic Species Concept (GSC)

Members of the same species will share the same genome (the entire genetic component of an organism, comprising all of its genes and DNA). This allows also identification of sister species.

Coyne summarizes the process of change by natural selection:

> Evolution by selection, then, is a combination of randomness and lawfulness. There is first a "random" (or "indifferent") process—the occurrence of mutations that generate an array of genetic variants, both good and bad (in the case of a mouse, a variety of new coat colors): and then a "lawful" process—natural selection—that orders this variation keeping the good and winnowing the bad (in a sand dunes mouse, light color genes increase at the expense of dark color one. (Coyne, 2009)

David Comings, our eminent geneticist author of chapter 14, has pointed out that this type of production of beneficial variants by single nucleotide mutations (STMs) is too rare and too slow to allow for macroevolution. He points out that DNA composed of repetitious sequences in the form of short tandem repeats (STRs) mutate a million to 10 million times faster than STMs. In addition, reusing or exchanging pieces of DNA already utilized in other contexts is responsible for most evolution. He summarizes a series of processes for rapid evolution (Comings 2008):

• Endosymbiosisian
• Whole genome duplication (polyploidy)
• Chromosomal rearrangements
• Gene duplication
• Hybridization
• Gene displacement

- Horizontal gene transfer
- Jumping genes
- Sexual recombination
- Retrotransposons (Alu sequences)
- Exon shuffling and domain exchange
- Repetitious DNA and repetitious peptides

This sort of new information, from a major authority, makes the fundamental changes necessary in the creation of new species, as opposed to the exhibition of fresh variations on an existing species, easier to conceive. Darwin knew nothing of genetics and so had to remain reticent on the possible mechanisms of speciation despite the brilliance of his intuitions.

Finding the Missing Links Or Rather Transitional Forms in the Fossil Record

Darwin was aware of the lack of proof for his theory in the fossil record of his time and we have narrated the much more recent doubting comments of Michael Denton. However new transitional forms are becoming available all the time which would have warmed Darwin's heart as exampled below:

- Lobe-finned fish to land dwelling amphibian tetra pod: Tiktaalik roseae.
- Reptile bipedal dinosaur to bird as in the recently discovered Chinese winged dinosaurs such as Micro raptor gui.
- Land dwelling mammals, such as Rodhocetus, going back to the water to lead to the evolution of modern whales.

These are regarded as transitional forms probably very close to true missing links. It is significant that Denton has softened his critical stance in his new book "Nature's Destiny."

RAMACHANDRAN: ANGELS TRAPPED IN THE BODIES OF BEASTS?

Vilanayanur Ramachandran is a charismatic physician and neuroscientist, who is director of the Center for Brain and Cognition at the University of California in San Diego. His 2011 book *The Tell-Tale Brain* looks at the subtleties of the human brain from an evolutionary viewpoint. He seeks the essential differences between man and ape particularly delving into man's unique concept of self and his or her special ability of introspection:

> Self-awareness is a trait that not only makes us human but para-
> doxically makes us want to be more than human. As I said in my
> Reith Lectures, "Science tells us we are merely beasts but we do not
> feel like that. We feel like angels trapped in the bodies of beasts,
> forever craving transcendence." That's the essential human predica-
> ment in a nutshell. (Ramachandran, 2011).

Dr Ramachandran sets out to list his intuitions as to what are the cardinal aspects of the self. He comes down to:

- Unity
- Continuity
- Embodiment
- Privacy
- Social embedding
- Free will
- Self-awareness

He asks himself how these multiple attributes of the self emerges in evolution, and he concludes that the development of the prefrontal cortex was
the key factor in its emergence.

Dr Ramachandran was once asked whether a non-anthropomorphic intelligence could lie behind the evolution of the extraordinary complexity of
the human brain. He responded as though it was a topic for his own reflections, replying that he could share a Spinoza-like viewpoint on life—Spinoza was, of course, a Pantheist equating god with nature, as we discussed
in the last chapter. He then quoted Shakespeare: "There are more things in
heaven and earth, Horatio, than are dreamt of in your philosophy."

He commented, however, that he saw no evidence of benevolence in the
system—shades of Tennyson's "nature red in tooth and claw."

Richard Dawkins, being asked whether he saw any evidence for intelligence guiding evolution, responded with a spirited rebuttal denying strongly that a recipe required intelligence. Natural selection, he said, could do it
all—shades of *The Blind Watchmaker*.

The Real Missing Link: What is the Impetus
behind the Evolutionary Process?

We can begin to see the extraordinary process of the evolution of life on
this planet as intuited by Darwin and now filled in by new findings and re-

search. Even the pragmatic Dawkins may describe aspects of it as wonderful and suggest that there could be an underlying recipe if not a blueprint. Plato would have felt that his forms were now plain to see, but Dawkins talks of "the dead hand of Plato," feeling that Plato's forms lack the dynamism of the natural selective process. Comings informs us that natural selection by simple beneficial mutations is too slow and too rare to explain speciation, as opposed to variations in a species. However, he demonstrates the amazing resources built into the genome to start to make the process feasible. But what drives this extraordinary machine: surely not pure chance, for the path from simple to complex and finally conscious forms of life is a clear pattern. Michael Behe saw intelligent design behind it, operated by a creationist deity but has progressively modified his views, as authorities like Francis Collins have shown that the central concept of "irreducibly complex" may not be justified. Also, he now seems concerned that the picture of his creationist deity may be hard to love when he or she or it has to be seen as responsible for such creations as the malarial parasite and the ichneumon fly. Darwin, much earlier, saw these implications, making him an agnostic at least.

Fred Hoyle saw not an anthropomorphic god behind the process but a cosmic intelligence. The information for the somewhat sporadic and initially painfully slow process was provided by genetic material from an ultimate source deep in the cosmos by the means of panspermia—an idea backed by such authorities as Arrhenius, Francis Crick and Paul Davies, with some qualifications. This would provide a cosmic stage for life rather than a purely earth-bound one. The miraculous chain of being has then been initiated by genetic seeds drifting into our planet's atmosphere.

In that case, where could the tree of origin lie? Can we ever endeavor to find our ultimate roots? Then we may be enabled to start to read the Braille of evolution and thereby enhance our intelligence to come to understand our selves much more fully. We may approach the ultimate intelligence and ponder its intentionality. A religion for life may emerge which does not need myth and magic to prop it up.

President Obama announced in April 2010 a new aim for NASA to send man to Mars. What clues may await us there? Any one day the receivers of SETI may wake up to evidence of extraterrestrial life. There is a missing link to explain the miracle of life. Could this be it? In the meantime, let us drink in the data of evolution as it floods into us and see what thought processes it triggers in us as a meditative species. We clearly stand on the shoulders of all pre-existing life forms. We must feel our debt to them in their struggle for existence and complexity. This can be a great stimulus to feel a new empathy with all forms of life both sentient and non sentient, for we are all of the same ultimate stuff. We may start to feel this with a religious intensity which overwhelms us. And a new type of ultimate meaning confronts us and we come home in This Strange Eventful History. The saving benefit of our final act, daunting though it may appear, should be the wisdom to appreciate the total miracle of life that we have been privileged to experience.

Reading List and Sources

Why Evolution is True. Jerry Coyne. Viking. 2009.

The Greatest Show On Earth. Richard Dawkins. Free Press. 2009.

Prehistoric Life. The Definitive Visual History Of Life On Earth. Senior Editors: Angeles Gavira Guerrero and Peter Frances. Dorling Kindersley. 2009.

BIBLIOGRAPHY

ABC & CBS News Polls on Evolution 2004.

Aristotle. "Nicomachean Ethics." *The Works of Aristotle Translated into English.* Oxford University Press. 1952.

Beauregard, Mario and O'Leary, Denyse. *The Spiritual Brain.* Harper One. 2007

Baring, Anne and Cashford, Jules. *The Myth of The Goddess. Evolution of An Image.* Viking Arkana.

Behe, Michael. *Darwin's Black Box.* Touchstone. 1996.

Behe, Michael. *The Edge of Evolution.* Free Press. 2007.

Bible. Deuteronomy 20:16, 17.

Boyer, Pascal. *Religion Explained.* Basic Books. 2001.

Burbridge, Jeffrey. *After Dinner Speech at Day of Celebration for Fred Hoyle's Contribution,* Cambridge 16 April 2002.

Carroll, Lewis. *Alice's Adventures in Wonderland.* Signet Classic. 2000.

Churchill Winston. *Painting as a Pastime.* Penguin Books. 1964.

Clinton, Bill. Speech by President Bill Clinton in the East Wing of the White House to celebrate completion of The Human Genome Project. 2000.

Collins, Francis. *The Language of God.* Free Press. 2006.

Comings, David. *Did Man Create God?* Hope Press. 2008.

Coyne, Jerry. *Why Evolution is True.* Viking. 2009

Cupitt, Don. *Life Life.* Polebridge Press. 2003.

Dalai Lama. *Freedom In Exile.* Hodder and Stoughton. 1990.

Darwin, Charles. *Autobiography*. 1887. Norton and Company. 1993.

Darwin, Charles. *Letter*.

Darwin, Charles: *Letter to Asa Gray*.

Davies, Paul. *The Fifth Miracle. The Search for the Origin and Meaning of Life*. Simon and Schuster. 1999.

Davies, Paul. *Cosmic Jackpot. Why Our Universe is Just Right for Life*. Houghton Mifflin. 2007.

Dawkins, Richard. *The Selfish Gene*. Oxford University Press. 1976.

Dawkins, Richard. *The Extended Phenotype*. Oxford University Press. 1982.

Dawkins, Richard. *The God Delusion*. Houghton Mifflin. 2006.

Dawkins, Richard. *The Greatest Show on Earth*. Free Press. 2009

De Chardin, Pierre Teilhard. *The Phenomenon of Man*. Fontana Religious Books. 1959.

De Waal, Frans. *Our Inner Ape*. Riverhead. 2005.

Dennett, Daniel. *Breaking the Spell. Religion as a Natural Phenomenon*. Viking. 2006.

Denton, Michael. *Evolution: A Theory in Crisis*. Adler and Adler. 1993.

Dostoevsky, Fyodor. *The Idiot*. 1868. Barnes and Noble Classics. 2004.

Eliade, Mircea. *The Sacred and the Profane: The Nature of Religion*, translated by William Trask. 1957.

Eliade, Mircea. *A History of Religious Ideas. Volume 3*. Preface. The University of Chicago Press. 1985.

Eliade, Mircea. *Autobiography. Volume 2. Exile's Odyssey*. Translated by Mac Linscolt Ricketts. The University of Chicago Press. 1988.

Eliade, Mircea. *Yoga*. Arkana Books. 1990.

Foucault, Michael. *The Archaeology of Knowledge*. 1969.Routledge. 1972.

Foucault, Michael. *History of Sexuality* 1954. Random House.1990.

Frankl, Viktor. *The Unheard Cry for Meaning*. Washington Square Press. 1978.

Frankl, Viktor. *Man's Search for Meaning*. Boston Press 1959, 2006.

Gandhi, Mahatma. *The Essential Writings of Mahatma Gandhi*. Edited by Raghavan Iyer. Oxford India Paperbacks. 1991.

Gauguin, Paul. "Interview with Jules Huret." *L'Echo de Paris*. 1891.

Gould, Stephen Jay. *Rock of Ages*. Ballantine Publishing Group. 1999.

Gould, Stephen Jay. *Wonderful Life: The Burgess Shale and the Nature of History*. Norton Paperback. 1990.

Gregory, Jane. *Fred Hoyle's Universe*. Oxford University Press. 2005.

Hick, John. *An Interpretation of Religion*. 1989. Revised Edition. Macmillan.

2004.

The Dalai Lama. *Freedom in Exile*. Hodder and Stoughton. 1990.

Hoyle, Fred. *The Intelligent Universe*. Michael Joseph Limited. 1983.

Hoyle, Fred. *The Black Cloud*. Penguin Books. 1957.

Hoyle, Fred. *Man and Materialism*. Ayer Company Publishing. 1957.

Hoyle, Fred and Chandra Wickramsinghe. *Our Place in the Cosmos*. J M Dent. 1993.

Hoyle, Fred. *Letter from Fred Hoyle to Bernard Lovell*. Quoted in his Obituary. Guardian. 2001.

Hume, David. *Enquiry Concerning Human Understanding* 1748. Oxford University Press. 1999.

Huxley, Aldous. *The Perennial Philosophy*. Harper Colophon. 1977.

Huxley, Julian and Kettlewell, HBD. *Charles Darwin and His World*. Thames and Hudson. 1974.

Jaeger, Werner. *Xenophanes. From the Theology of the Early Greek Philosophers*. 1936. Wipf and Stock. 2003.

Jaspers, Karl. *The Origin and Goal of History* 1953. Greenwood Press. 1977.

Jung, Carl. *Memories, Dreams, Reflections*. Recorded and edited by A. Jaffe. Pantheon Books. 1963.

Kant, Immanuel. *The Metaphysics of Morals* 1785. Oxford University Press. 2002.

Kauffman, Stuart. *Reinventing The Sacred*. Basic Books.2008

Keats, John: *Letters of John Keats*. Harvard University Press. 2002.

King, Barbara. *Evolving God*. Doubleday. 2007.

Lawrence, David Herbert. *Lady Chatterley's Lover*.1928.Modern Library. 1993.

Lovell, Bernard. *Obituary to Fred Hoyle*. Guardian. 23 August 2001.

Lehigh University. The Department of Biological Sciences of Lehigh University: *Official Position Statement*. 1998.

MacLean, Paul. *The Triune Brain in Evolution*. Plenum. 1990.

Majjima, Nikaya. *The Buddha*. Collections of discourses in The Pali Canon.

Mehrotra, Rajiv (edited by). *The Essential Dalai Lama: His Important Teachings*. Chapter 13. A Wish for Harmony. Viking Press. 2005.

Norton, W.W and Porter, Roy. *Hippocrates. From The Greatest Benefit to Human Kind. A Medical History of Humanity*. 1999.

O'Leary, Denyse and Beauregard, Mario. *The Spiritual Brain*. Harper One. 2007

Parrinder, Geoffrey. *The Bhagavad Gita: A Verse Translation*. Sheldon Press. 1974.

Persinger, Michael. "Experimental Stimulation of the God Experience." In

Neurotheology. Edited by R. Joseph. University Press California. 2003.

Pirsig, Robert. *Zen and the Art of Motorcycle Maintenance*. A Bantam Book. 1981.

Pope Pius XII. Encyclical Humani Generis. 1950.

Pope John Paul II to the Pontificial Academy of Sciences entitled "*Truth Cannot Contradict Truth*". 1996.

Prigogine, Ilya. *The End of Certainty*. 1997.

Primack,Joel & Abrams, Nancy. *The View from the Center of the Universe*. Riverhead Books.2006.

Ramachandran V. S. *The Tell-Tale Brain–A Neuroscientist's Quest for What Makes Us Human*. W. W. Norton and Company. 2011.

Ratzinger, Joseph Cardinal: Reported in the Catholic Origins, CNS Documentary Service (Vol 26, No. 20, 31st October) 1996.

Rees, Martin. *Obituary to Fred Hoyle*. Physics Today. 2001. 54.72.

Sartre, Jean-Paul. *Nausea*. Translated from the French by Lloyd Alexander 1938. New Directions Paperbook. 2007.

Schopenhauer, Arthur. *The World as Will and Representation*. 1818. Dover Publications. 1969.

Schopenhauer, Arthur. *Supplement to Book 4 Ch xli*. Ditto. 1818.

Schwartz, Gary and Simon, William. *The G.O.D. Experiments*. Antra Books. 2006.

Shakespeare, William. *As You Like It*. Act II, Scene 7.

Shakespeare, William. *As You Like It*.Act II, Scene 1.

Shakespeare, William. *Macbeth*. Act V, Scene 19.

Shakespeare, William. *The Tempest*. Act V, Epilogue.

Shakespeare, William. *The Tempest*. Act III, Scene 3.

Shakespeare, William. *Hamlet*. Act I, Scene 3.

Schwartz, Gary and Simon, William. *The G.O.D. Experiments*. Antra Books. 2006.

Teasdale, Wayne.*The Mystic Heart. Discovering a Universal Spirituality in the World's Religions*. Foreword by the Dalai Lama. New World Library. 1999.

Tennyson, Alfred Lord. *In Memoriam A.H.H. Poem*. 1850.

Terkel, Studs. *Hope Dies Last*. New Press. 2003.

Van Gogh, Vincent. Letter to his brother Theo. April 1885.

Van Gogh, Vincent. Letter to his brother Theo. January 1889.

Van Gogh, Vincent. *The Passionate Eye*. Pascal Bonafoux. Thames and Hudson. 1992.

Vatican II: Documents Related to Papal Statement *Redemptor Hominis* 1979. Discussion.

Wilson, David Sloan. *Evolution for Everyone*. A Delacorte Book. 2007.